"I've never been one to wear h.... is too big, but that's another story. However, Dr. Gary McIntosh has helped me realize that to lead more effectively as a pastor I must wear various hats. In this book, hats represent the roles of a pastor, and I've never seen them defined so clearly. This book will help you lead better as soon as you engage it. We will be studying the book as a staff, and I encourage you to take a deep dive into the wisdom of my good friend Dr. McIntosh. Now that I think about it, I've never tried on a cowboy hat. I wonder if they have one in my size . . ."

Dr. Nelson Searcy, author and founding/teaching pastor,
The Journey Church, New York City

"Pastors bearing a heavy load of demands and pressures have just been given a gift! This book simplifies the work of leading a church and is a practical tool for moving into an uncertain future."

Tom Harper, publisher, BiblicalLeadership.com;
author of *Servant Leader Strong: Uniting Biblical
Wisdom and High-Performance Leadership*

"Gary is known as a down-to-earth writer who provides principles that any pastor can use. He does not disappoint in this book. All pastors would agree with the ten key roles he identifies. The illustrations he shares come from his wealth of experience working with churches of all sizes. You will find the information about prioritizing your hats very helpful in implementing the insights provided."

Dr. Phil Stevenson, district superintendent, PSW Movement

"This book is destined to be a pastoral preparation classic, as McIntosh defines ten critical roles of today's pastor. The book is brimming with telling research, provocative stories, and sage wisdom. Reading his synthesis on leadership hats will set hearts afire and minds spinning on how to lead the church more effectively.

Some of the mirroring illustrations may be potent enough to help you avoid pastoral pitfalls and launch you into bigger and better mission trajectories. The 'Dr. Mc Sez' sections cut through the haze with straight talk. Get it. Read it. Apply it. Work it into your life and picture. You won't regret it!"

Gary Comer, author of *Soul Whisperer* and *ReMission*; president of Soul Whisperer Ministry

"Pastoring a church is not for the faint of heart! This book reflects the complexity of the pastor's role. It is a treasure of guidance based on both knowledge and experience. A must-read for those preparing for ministry, and a wise read for every functioning pastor. Dr. McIntosh provides a lifetime of priceless direction for every pastor and church leader."

Kent R. Hunter, church consultant, Church Doctor Ministries; author of *Restoring Civility: Lessons from the Master*

the
10 Key Roles
of a Pastor

the
10 Key Roles
of a Pastor

Proven Practices for Balancing
the Demands of Leading Your Church

Gary L. McIntosh

BakerBooks

a division of Baker Publishing Group
Grand Rapids, Michigan

Published by Baker Books
a division of Baker Publishing Group
PO Box 6287, Grand Rapids, MI 49516-6287
www.bakerbooks.com

Printed in the United States of America

Library of Congress Cataloging-in-Publication Data
Names: McIntosh, Gary, 1947– author.
Title: The 10 key roles of a pastor : proven practices for balancing the demands of leading your church / Gary L. McIntosh.
Other titles: Ten key roles of a pastor
Description: Grand Rapids, Michigan : Baker Books, a division of Baker Publishing Group, [2021]
Identifiers: LCCN 2020042380 | ISBN 9780801094880 (paperback) | ISBN 9781540901675 (casebound)
Subjects: LCSH: Clergy—Office.
Classification: LCC BV660.3 .M345 2021 | DDC 253—dc23
LC record available at https://lccn.loc.gov/2020042380

Hat Designs by Pert Alacar of *Comics Alacarte*

Some names and details have been changed to protect the privacy of the individuals involved.

21 22 23 24 25 26 27   7 6 5 4 3 2 1

Contents

What Pastors Do

What do pastors actually do? While the answer may seem obvious to many, others ask the question with honest curiosity. It is difficult to explain to people what a pastor does all week. From the viewpoint of some, the pastor works only on Sunday. In point of fact, of course, this mindset is completely inaccurate. My research shows that pastors work an average of sixty-three hours a week on various aspects of ministry. However, what a pastor actually does during that time is complex, subtle, and difficult to express.

Being a pastor is an engaging job, at once supported by over two thousand years of tradition, while challenged by the changing face of today's culture. Advancing technology opens doors of innovation, new philosophies call for fresh approaches to communication, and changing generations bring new expectations. It's an intriguing job with endless opportunities to do good. It's by far one of the most fascinating jobs I know—a job that makes a great deal of difference in the lives of people for now and for eternity.

As a trainer of future pastors at Talbot School of Theology, Biola University, for the past thirty-five years, I've found that students preparing for pastoral ministry think they'll wear only one hat—the speaker's hat! Such students place high value on classes like biblical studies, languages, and homiletics, while slighting courses on church management, leadership, and general pastoral skills. Yet, as most experienced pastors realize, time spent each week on teaching and preaching is quite minimal compared to the other demands that come their way. Congregations expect their pastors to spend time setting the church's direction, providing care and counsel, and working for organizational effectiveness. The hats cover a multitude of approaches, challenges, and opportunities unique to each person. Nevertheless, hats are made to be worn, and successful pastors wear them.

Pastors come from nearly anywhere today. Historically, most pastors came from small churches located in smaller communities. They were trained in Bible schools, colleges, and seminaries before joining the ranks of dedicated clergy. Over the last half century, age-old barriers have deteriorated. Pastors now come from larger churches and larger communities. Many young women, as well as men, now aspire to (and some do) lead congregations. A significant number of middle-aged people enter pastoral ministry with years of experience in various fields of work. However, I sometimes wonder if these future pastors understand what all is involved in ministry.

Pastors can, do, and must wear many different hats in their work. Each hat represents a role. Pastors shift roles in a matter of a few minutes. One moment they are activists, the next counselors, and the next managers. I remember wearing four different hats in a matter of just a few hours when I was a pastor. Sunday morning I wore the speaker's hat. Immediately after the worship service I wore the counselor's hat while talking with a middle-aged couple in my office. Later that afternoon, in a meeting with the board, I wore the executive's hat, and that evening I wore the reporter's hat as I spoke at a neighborhood meeting. Many are the days when pastors wear all the hats. I know there were days when I wore them all. One day I counted up all the hats I wore during the week, and it came to ten: speaker, captain, coach, executive, director, counselor, student, pioneer, conductor, and reporter. Pastors are involved with nearly every role known to humanity, for which many have little training.

In this book, I introduce, explain, and demonstrate how all ten hats must be part of each pastor's wardrobe if they are to lead a church fruitfully into the future. No pastor wears every hat equally well, but I'll show you how to make maximum use of each hat in your ministry. If you're not a pastor, this book will help you as you lead any organization. If you can improve the way you wear the ten hats of a pastor, you will put into action proven procedures and practices for making your church, ministry, or organization as fruitful as possible.

So, glance over the ten hats in the table of contents, or simply scan through each chapter. Start reading about the hat that interests you, or challenges you, or presents struggles for you. Start applying the insights and actions described in that chapter. By doing so, you will put into action strategies for fruitful ministry.

Gary L. McIntosh, Temecula, CA

1

The Speaker's Hat

Hats, hats, and more hats. Look around as you walk down the street, and you'll see people wearing numerous types of hats. Many hats, perhaps most, are just an expression of personal style. Some, of course, convey allegiance to a sports team, and others signal that a person is employed in a particular field. For example, you might spot a person wearing a yellow plastic hard hat. In most situations, you'd be correct to assume the person worked in construction. Yellow hard hats are regularly worn in that job to protect the worker from harmful objects.

If you look at pictures from years ago, you'll see it was quite common for public speakers to wear a top hat. Presidents Abraham Lincoln, Teddy Roosevelt, and John Kennedy regularly wore a top hat as they made their way to places where they were to speak. The practice of wearing top hats has disappeared in recent years as people embraced more casual styles. Even presidents have selected different hats to wear. Ronald Reagan and George W. Bush regularly wore cowboy hats, for example. However, the top hat represents a speaker and is used here to depict the speaker or preacher.

The speaker's hat is the most visible hat worn by all pastors. Every time pastors preach, lead a study, speak at an event, or in some way address people, they put it on. Pastors in growing churches average ten hours a week wearing this hat, which includes preparation time for any speaking events. They spend five hours more per week (twice as much) wearing this hat as do pastors in declining churches, and three hours (43 percent) more per week than pastors in plateaued churches. For many people, perhaps most, this is the only hat they ever see the pastor wearing. Since church attendees primarily see pastors in this hat, they tend to judge them by their ability to communicate.

Preach the Word

Pastors and preaching—they go together like peanut butter and jelly. Church members rarely extend a call or accept an appointment of a pastor without first hearing them preach. If you hear others discussing the strengths and weaknesses of a pastor, the criterion is most often their preaching skill. Even the apostle Paul evaluated his ministry based somewhat on his preaching and teaching. When leaving the Ephesian church, Paul told the elders, "I did

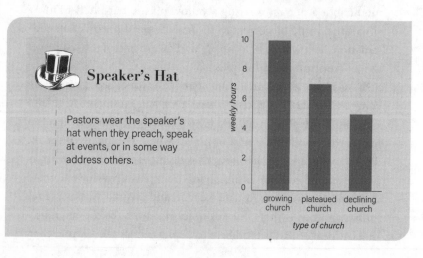

Speaker's Hat

Pastors wear the speaker's hat when they preach, speak at events, or in some way address others.

not shrink from declaring to you anything that was profitable, and teaching you publicly and from house to house. . . . I did not shrink from declaring to you the whole purpose of God" (Acts 20:20, 27). Later he exhorted Timothy to "preach the word" (2 Tim. 4:2), a command taken to heart by all pastors ever since.

Speaking is an important aspect of any pastor's ministry. It is the first hat on the rack! All pastors rank the speaker's hat as the primary one they wear weekly.

The Case of the Confused Pastor. Pastor Carl Robinson started Faith Baptist Church right after graduating from Bible college. His personable style, which included what he called a "gift of gab," enabled the church to grow quickly in its first year from a launch team of 27 to 130 worshipers by the beginning of the church's second year. He spent a great amount of time caring for the members of his congregation, which endeared him to their hearts. His Sunday sermons were not always the best, and members of the congregation were heard to make comments like, "Pastor Carl hit a double today." He had often used a baseball analogy to explain his preaching, saying, "Well, I hit a home run today." Or, when the sermon wasn't so good, "I hit a single today." The people knew Pastor Carl loved them and forgave the low quality of his sermons. As the church continued to increase in size over the next few years, Pastor Carl noticed a changing attitude among the people regarding his preaching. He observed less laughter when he jokingly said, "I only hit a single today." People still seemed to enjoy his personal visits and conversations over coffee at local restaurants, but he had no doubt that they were less accepting of his sermons. He couldn't understand the change. It was puzzling.

What Pastor Carl experienced is a natural occurrence. The larger a church grows, the more important the speaker's hat becomes. In larger churches, people don't have the same level of personal relationship with the pastor, which means they are usually less forgiving if a sermon is not prepared or delivered well. No longer are they satisfied with the pastor hitting a single or double. Since the Sunday sermon is what they primarily know about the pastor, they expect a triple or home run each week. While wearing the speaker's hat is important for every pastor, it is crucial for pastors in larger churches. As a church increases in size, the pastor's sermons must also improve.

Can pastors become better preachers? Yes, they can. If you want your church to grow, you must improve. Good preaching, of course, depends on a number of factors. Here are some ideas to help you hit more triples and home runs each week.

Know Your God

One of the words used for leader in the Old Testament (Hebrew: *nagid*, root *nagad*) is translated by several English words, including captain, ruler, prince, governor, noble, officer, and official. Basically, it means that the kind of leader God desires for his people is a person who (1) knows him, (2) knows his desires, and (3) announces his desires to others.

The Case of the Uncertain Pastor. First Presbyterian Church was once a larger congregation of eight hundred people located just across the river from New York City. After fifty-seven years of fruitful ministry, it experienced a decade of decline, which raised numerous questions about its future. The congregation naturally looked to its long-standing pastor, Mike Bruce, for answers. Unfortunately, Reverend Mike was quite uncertain about both the church's direction as well as his own. One Sunday he ended his sermon with the following comment: "Folks, I wish I could be more certain about the direction of our church, but I'm not even sure I'm going to heaven." As you might expect, his comment created a major furor in the congregation. Many called the elders and asked, "If our pastor isn't even sure of his own salvation, how can he lead us?" It was a good question, indeed.

Pastors have all been taught, in one way or another, techniques or processes for putting a sermon together. Finding a formula for experiencing the awe or special anointing or work of the Holy

Spirit in a sermon is akin to trying to find the smell of a rose by pulling off each petal.

Older pastors used to call this mysterious aspect *unction.* All pastors need some sort of process for putting together their sermons, but if a pastor doesn't know God personally and deeply, nothing is likely to happen.

Know Yourself

If you really know God, then you must consider yourself in the light of his attributes. In doing so, you realize your personal failure to live up to God's standards and your own need of forgiveness and redemption. Thus, you come to the sermon *as one who needs the Savior.* The tone of your sermon inevitably reflects this knowledge, as you appropriately admit your own struggle with living the Christian life. The sermon then projects an air of authenticity rather than superiority. It communicates a feel of humility rather than pride. It presents an aura of reality rather than pretense. You also must come to the sermon *as one who has the Savior.* Knowing yourself means you know not only your weaknesses and failures but also the liberty, hope, and joy found from embracing the Savior's redemption. You can stand in the pulpit knowing your frailties but also the Savior's grace. Thus, you preach as a *participant* in the message rather than as a *performer* of the message. Instead of hiding your weaknesses (performing), you allow your personality to come out (participating), knowing that God applies his Word to human hearts through an authentic messenger. It is glorious to be yourself. Preaching really is delivering truth through personality.

Know Your Text

Pastors typically don't find exegesis challenging. They can work their way through the scriptural text, get the flow of thought, and understand the context. They know the basics of sermon preparation: choose the text, determine what it means, meditate on it, isolate the dominant thought, arrange the material to serve the dominant thought, add the introduction and conclusion, etc. It all begins with the text. Understanding it is paramount. What's much more difficult, of course, is determining, "What does it mean today?" Knowing the text implies both accurately exegeting it and letting it touch your own life. Good preaching arises out of wrestling with the text—thinking about it and experiencing it in some fashion. How has it touched your own life? Where have you seen it worked out in others' lives? Preaching is not merely repeating the first idea that comes out of a commentary or out of a respected leader's mouth; the idea must come out of your critical study of the text, which is then applied to real life. Knowing the text is a two-sided coin: knowing what it meant to the original writer, and then knowing what it means to people today. Stuart Briscoe, a respected pastor, discloses, "I like to live in a message for a week until it becomes as comfortable as a pair of old slippers."[1]

Know Your Audience

Good sermons are sermons that do good. The major league of preaching is seeing people change their lives to become more like Jesus. So, focus on doing good with your sermons, not on preaching great sermons.

Be aware of the questions people are asking. Each generation asks different questions. Younger people in their twenties want to know how they are uniquely created by God, particularly how they are different from their families of origin. They desire to know where to center their lives—around God, work, friends, etc. Thirty-year-olds face serious responsibilities—mortgages, spouses, babies, in-law relationships, and work stressors. They have many questions revolving around these aspects of life. For people in their forties, they wonder about career and marriage disappointments. Should they scale back their dreams or forge ahead? By their fifties, people wonder if they're past their prime. Few friendships, children leaving the home, and less-than-satisfying jobs force unexpected feelings to the surface. Some fight feelings of loss, search for intimacy in wrong places, and wonder if they bring value to anyone any longer. Those in their sixties wonder what it means to be old, if they look as old as their peers, and how to deal with long-term resentments. For people in their seventies and beyond, questions arise as to how long they have left on this earth, how to maintain their independence as they grow older, and what will happen to the family when they're gone.

The pastor must know the people to address these fears, inadequacies, and regrets. This requires pastors to have a deep love for the people. It's impossible to preach well if you don't love your people. If you can't peer into their eyes and see their hurt and lostness, you have little right to preach the gospel to them. Pastoring is never impersonal. If you are in a smaller church, it's likely that you know everyone fairly well. On the other hand, if you're in a larger church, where it's impossible to know all the people, you must know some of them well enough to speak to their pains, struggles, and hopes. When pastors first come out of seminary or Bible school, they end up preaching to their professors. Some are still preaching to their professors after years of being a pastor. Preach to your people. Let them see that you know and understand what they need to follow Christ in their world.

Other Factors That Impact Sermon Preparation

Other factors, of course, affect how a pastor prepares a sermon. Experience has a major impact on the time necessary to prepare a sermon, with younger pastors typically taking longer, and more experienced pastors needing less time. The genre being preached affects preparation time. Is the message from a Psalm or a passage in Revelation? Some parts of the Bible are just easier to get a handle on, thus take less time to develop. Regardless of the topic, time, or context, "we preach Christ crucified" (1 Cor. 1:23).

DR. MC SEZ

Excellent preaching is more of an art than a science, but I've discovered a few tips over the years.

- **Good preachers prepare.** I have found that the best preachers spend about fifteen hours in sermon preparation, divided over two weeks. In the first week, the pastor spends about seven to eight hours exegeting the passage(s) of Scripture in order to understand it. The big idea or eternal principle is defined, and a tentative outline is prepared. Many pastors will then let the message percolate for a week of prayerful reflection. The following week, an additional seven to eight hours are given to filling out the outline with illustrations, stories, testimonies, and other didactic techniques, as well as practicing the delivery.
- **Good preachers preach twenty to thirty minutes; bad preachers shouldn't preach any longer.** I recall the late Haddon Robinson, a world-renowned expert on preaching, writing, "Some men preach for an hour and it seems like twenty minutes, and some preach for twenty minutes and it seems like an hour. I wonder what the difference is?" That's a wonderful question. Every pastor would do well to seek an answer to it.
- **Good preachers practice.** The great soccer player Pelé was asked how he defined success. Reportedly, he said something like, "Success isn't how many games you win but how hard you practice after you lose." One pastor I know took Pelé's definition to heart. Each Friday and Saturday, he'd go into the auditorium when no one was around and preach his entire sermon to empty seats—six times! Yes, six times he preached the entire sermon, making changes, corrections, and adjustments. By the time he stood up on Sunday morning to preach, it was his seventh time! People thought his ability to catch their attention in the introduction, lead them through a well-thought-out message, and end with a thoughtful challenge was a natural gift. What they didn't know or see was his practice. Preachers who wear the speaker's hat well put in the time. They practice.
- **Good preachers are interesting.** If you're going to bore people, bore them with Shakespeare, not the Bible. Fruitful preachers live with a

fear of boring people, that is, making the Bible and God—which are relevant—irrelevant. Boredom is difficult for people to tolerate. Instead of drawing people to God, boring sermons drive them from him. God is not boring, so why should your sermons be?

- **Good preachers entertain people.** I've heard critics say we shouldn't entertain people, but I'd like to file a minority report here. Entertainment means "to hold one's attention," which I think all speakers desire to do. What you should not do is amuse people, which means "to be without thought." Keep people's attention, but make sure to keep them thinking.

- **Good preachers listen to their people.** Some church members will give you feedback or offer criticism. They most likely lack the preaching experience and training to diagnose problems and prescribe how to help you preach better. But their comments may point out an issue that you need to hear and address. Listen to what they are saying.

- **Good preachers offer solutions.** They spend more time giving answers than pointing out problems. I get it. It's easier to show others what's wrong than to offer solutions. It's a problem/solution issue. Many pastors spend twice as much time on describing the problem as on the solution. Make sure your most powerful illustrations and descriptions show people what to do. An old Christian saint, Francis de Sales, once noted, "The test of a preacher is that his congregation goes away saying, not 'What a lovely sermon!' but 'I will do something.'"

- **Good preachers condition themselves.** Preparing a sermon is different than preparing yourself. No good long-distance runner attempts a marathon without conditioning their body ahead of time. Neither should a pastor step into the pulpit, or on the stage, without prior conditioning. Personal submission to the Lord throughout the week is a must. Prayer, journaling, fasting, solitude, reflection, and meditation help condition you for delivering God's Word to the people.

Preaching is a challenge in today's environment. The world has people around 110 hours a week (168 total hours minus about 56 hours for sleeping and maybe 2 hours for church). We're in a time disparity wilderness, trying to be heard amongst the noises of a thousand other voices. Many times you won't see anything happening week to week, but God is working unseen under the surface in people's lives. It's the Spirit of God who enlivens those who hear your preaching. It's similar to eating three meals a day. Most of us cannot remember what we ate last week or even yesterday. Sure, we can remember an occasional fantastic meal, but most meals don't create any lasting memories. Yet, we'd be considered impoverished if we hadn't had the opportunity to eat three meals a day every day over the last year. It's good to remember that preaching is like that too. People normally don't change dramatically every Sunday. However, your faithful preaching of God's Word works over time to move people in the right way.

It's also good to remember that your sufficiency for preaching is in God. From time to time, it's common for pastors to feel like failures or even like hypocrites. Preaching the Word of God challenges your life all the time. When pastors preach about commitment, they ask themselves, "How committed am I?" If they preach about sacrifice, they ask themselves, "How sacrificial am I?" If they preach about forgiveness, they ask themselves, "How forgiving am I?"

Like Paul, pastors always ask quietly in their hearts, "Who is adequate for these things?" (2 Cor. 2:16). The answer, of course, is no one. Except Paul declares that "our adequacy is from God" (3:5). Where does such adequacy arise? Paul says, "We are not like many, peddling the word of God" (2:17). We do not adulterate the word of God (4:2), "for we do not preach ourselves but Christ Jesus as Lord" (4:5). When wearing the speaker's hat, pastors always have total inability but overwhelming adequacy.

Build Your Ethos

You may not like to acknowledge it, but people in your church have an opinion of you. Hopefully most see you as credible, which means you have high *ethos*. The concept of ethos refers to the perceived credibility of the speaker. If your ethos is poor, people will turn you off before you speak. If your ethos is high, people will be anxious to listen and learn from your every word.

At its basic level, ethos is determined by your character and your competency. Both are seen in the life of King David, as reported in Psalm 78:72. David is described as a shepherd who guided Israel with character—"according to the integrity of his heart"—and with competency—"with his skillful hands." This is a hopeful commentary, for it lets us know we don't have to exhibit perfect character. David wasn't perfect, as is well known, but he had the integrity to confess his sins and trust in God's guidance (2 Sam. 12:13–25). He also had the skill to oversee the government of Israel, lead the army, and guide the nation into a time of prosperity.

Listeners respond to and learn from a pastor they like and trust. You can wear the speaker's hat well if you build your competency and character. Studies have found that trust is gained with speakers who have an attractive appearance, a fluent delivery, and an organized message (competency).

Our society's acceptance of casual dress has infiltrated many churches. It's not unusual in some church settings to see worship leaders, teams, and pastors dressed anywhere from casual, dressy clothes to an extreme bordering on sloppiness. It is argued, of course, that dress (and overall grooming) is not a true indicator of competency. This is right, but in their minds, listeners do make a connection. My advice is to always dress a little nicer than those in the audience; always groom yourself a little better than those in the congregation. It just makes sense, and it will raise the credibility factor in the minds of your people. Knowing your material and practicing it enough so that you can speak it fluently will also help your congregation to trust your message. However, if you *uh* struggle to find words for *uh* expressing your *uh* feelings, you'll lower your credibility in the eyes of your listeners. If your sermons are easy to follow and have clear structure, people will say, "I understand what you're saying." Conversely, if people comment, "I have no idea what you just said," you're in trouble. You can raise your level of trust and credibility in the eyes and minds of your people if you communicate an aura of excellence through your appearance, delivery, and the organization of your message.

The other important aspect of building credibility is communicating character. David was described first as a person with character and second as a person of competence. Perhaps this order of words was not an accident but signals the importance of character in the life of a leader. From the time of Aristotle, it's been accepted that a person's character is likely their most persuasive power. Thus, if you want people to listen to your message, you must demonstrate character. In the mind of the listeners, this means they can say with confidence, "I like you, and I know you like me." When you wear the speaker's hat, your people's belief that you love them is influenced 7 percent by the content of your message, 38 percent by your tone of voice, and 55 percent by your facial expressions.[2] For preachers, this is profound. If people in the congregation like you, they will tend to listen to you and follow your directions. If they don't like you, they will not listen to you or put your sermons into practice. Likability comes down to two aspects: absence of pride and love for your people. Absence of pride is perceived when you focus on building God's kingdom rather than your own, when you lift up others rather than yourself, and when you give others praise while you take the blame. Loving your people is observed as you smile and talk with a kind tone of voice. A pastor should always walk slowly through the lobby, smiling and talking lovingly with people along the way. If you do these few simple actions, your people will say, "My pastor likes me."

Communicate So People Remember

Research indicates that people remember less than 10 percent of the unsupported spoken word.[3] Yet, Sunday after Sunday, pastors stand behind pulpits, sit next to tables, or walk across stages employing the weakest approach to communication. Few church attendees can answer yes to the simple question, "Do you remember the pastor's sermon from two weeks ago?"

Yet, you can do much so that your message can be recalled. Here are some ideas to use to raise the level of remembrance.

First, know how people learn. Keep in mind the two main principles by which people learn: through redundancy and multisensory communication. *Redundancy* means we learn when exposed to a message more than one time. *Multisensory communication* means we learn when exposed to a message in more than one way.

Second, get people's attention and hold it. One question people are always asking is, "What's in it for me?" What gets and holds their attention is what they fear (e.g., loss of a job, death of a loved one, a major illness, etc.), what is unexpected (e.g., riding into an auditorium on a motorcycle, a well-known surprise guest, question and answer time as part of the sermon, etc.), and what is valued (e.g., knowing God's will, deepening relationships, cherished memories, etc.). Trying to get attention with the unexpected leads to the use of gimmicks, which must be bigger and better each week. Obviously, that's not the best way to gain attention nor hold it. The other two are better, as they speak to concerns and important values. Determine your people's values and concerns. Then look for what the Bible says about them, and ask and answer real questions about those values and concerns.

Third, employ memory tools. You can enhance your people's retention of the message through visualization, drama, storytelling, and testimonies.

- *Visualization*: Projecting the key words and phrases of your sermon on a screen helps sear them into the minds of your listeners. Using a projector to outline the sermon, highlight Scripture, integrate appropriate video clips, and show purposeful cartoons adds additional visual stimuli so people not only hear your words but also see them with their eyes.

- *Drama*: The most helpful use of drama is to illustrate a problem in three to five minutes for which the sermon provides a solution. While scripts are available for purchase from major Christian publishing companies, in the long run, the drama scripts that churches write themselves fit the message they wish to communicate more clearly.

- *Storytelling*: Jesus was a master storyteller. He knew that a story could capture his listeners' attention and help them remember his message. A story is similar to an illustration in that it takes listeners into the realm of their imagination—a powerful and engaging part of the mind. While an illustration clarifies a point, a story makes a point, and the sermon clarifies it.

- *Testimonies*: Allowing people to share their personal stories of changed lives has long been practiced in churches. Historically, time in worship services was dedicated for testimonies in many churches. With recording and projection systems in use by most churches today, filming testimonies and playing them on large screens provides an even greater impact. As people in the congregation look into the faces of people sharing stories of loss and redemption, the power of testimony undergirds the sermon dramatically.

Fourth, repeat the primary change you wish to see. One reason people are unimpressed by sermons and forget them is that pastors don't know why they're preaching a particular sermon. If someone asks a pastor why they are preaching a sermon, they might answer, "I was in Ephesians 1 last week, and I'm in Ephesians 2 this week." Pastors rarely ask, "How do I expect people to change as a result of this sermon?" If you're not preaching for a response, your message will be flat. It will lack emotion and power. Always ask, "What do I want my people to do when I'm done?" Then use the principle of redundancy by repeating what you want people to do multiple times throughout your message.

DR. MC SEZ

Wearing the speaker's hat requires that you know what you know and are aware of the world around you. Listeners believe the preaching of a pastor who knows their job and who is likewise knowledgeable about the listeners' interests. People trust a pastor who is aware of their world: jobs, personal situations, schools, families, and news. Being aware of happenings around you demonstrates to your people that you understand them, their challenges, and their opportunities. At the least, this means being a reader of more than blogs and listening to more than podcasts. Most blogs and podcasts reflect the opinions of others, which are most often not vetted for accuracy or content. Reading solid books and articles, as well as listening to documented teachers and pastors, is needed more than ever in our society. Having a wide-ranging familiarity with life, government, local and national issues, and human life shows up in your preaching, allowing listeners to perceive you as likeable and credible.

Wearing the speaker's hat requires a pastor to communicate in numerous ways besides preaching. Yet, it is the most visible hat to those in the congregation, and it must be worn well. It's called a top hat for a reason—it's the top hat on the pastor's rack.

For Further Reading

Classic: Haddon W. Robinson. *Biblical Preaching: The Development and Delivery of Expository Messages*. 3rd ed. Grand Rapids: Baker Academic, 2014.

Newer: Donald Sunukjian. *Invitation to Biblical Preaching: Proclaiming Truth with Clarity and Relevance*. Grand Rapids: Kregel Academic, 2007.

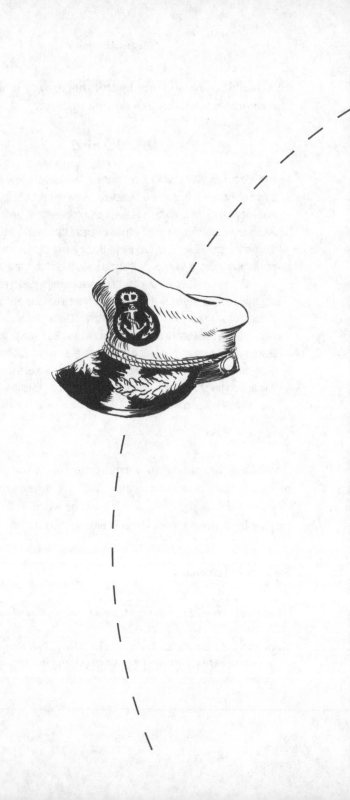

2

The Captain's Hat

It is often said that everything rises or falls on leadership. If that is true, and I believe it is, then it's important to discover who leads a church. Note that I didn't ask, "Who is the leader of the church?" The clear answer to that question, of course, is Jesus Christ. He alone builds his church (Matt. 16:18); he alone is the head of the church (Eph. 1:22); he alone is the chief shepherd (1 Pet. 5:4).

Who Leads the Church?

The question I pose is, "Who leads a church?" In my experience, churches are led in four primary ways (with numerous variations): by congregation, board/committee, team, or pastor.

Congregation

Quite a number of churches in the United States look to the total congregation for leadership. The general theological rationale for this approach is to respect the truth that the Holy Spirit indwells all true believers (Rom. 8:9; 1 Cor. 3:16; 6:19). The Holy Spirit empowers each believer in the congregation for life (Gal. 5:22–23) and service (1 Cor. 12:4–13; 1 Pet. 4:10). Thus, it seems logical to allow the congregation to lead through some means of democratic action (such as voting, congregational meetings, or similar activities), by which the Holy Spirit speaks through the full congregation of believers. Some theologians support this approach by pointing out that the early church demonstrated this type of leadership by voting on the seven men who took over the task of distributing food to widows (Acts 6:3–6). This approach fits North American culture well with its culture of democratic individualism, in which everyone has a say or vote. It is no surprise that quite a few churches feel that Jesus Christ leads his church through congregational decisions.

Board/Committee

Some churches follow the practice of allowing the congregation to select its leaders to serve on boards or committees, which then give direction to the church. This approach also finds support in the actions of the first congregation in Acts 6, who selected seven leaders and then, supposedly, found them working as a board/committee to design a better system to serve food to the widows. The board/committee concept is ingrained in some church circles so deeply that the seven leaders are regularly referred to as deacons (the twelve being seen as the elders), even though neither group is called that in the text. It also fits well with the directions given to the church for elders and deacons (1 Tim. 3:1–13; Titus 1:5–9), the exhortation of Paul to the elders in Ephesus to take responsible leadership (Acts 20:28–35), and the command to the Hebrews to obey their leaders (Heb. 13:17). The board/committee approach also fits well with North American corporate structure in which for-profit and nonprofit corporations function with boards of directors and subcommittees.

Team

Over the past few years, there has been a gradual trend toward team ministry. In a few churches, notably larger ones, this trend involves the development of an executive team of pastors who work together to lead a church. Voices from several arenas now promote the use of multiple preachers rather than relying on just one pastor. By having two or three pastors preach, it is argued, the power of individual personality is limited, while the Bible is exegeted in more balanced ways. Furthermore, by having a team of pastors lead the church, excesses of ambition or exuberance are mitigated.

Support for using teams is found in both the Old and New Testaments. Moses operated with a team comprised of Aaron, Hur, and Joshua (Exod. 4:14–16; 17:8–13). King David surrounded himself with Zadok, Abiathar, Hushai, and Ziba (2 Sam. 15:24–16:4). Jesus and his disciples (especially Peter, James, and John) resemble a team in many ways (Matt. 10:1; Mark 3:14; 6:31–32; Luke 6:11–16; 9:1). Even though we think of the apostle Paul as a dominant person, he also worked with a team. His coworkers included Barnabas, John Mark, Timothy, Luke, Titus, Prisca and Aquila, and Silas (Acts 15:40; 19:22; Rom. 16:3–4, 21; Col. 4:7–14; 2 Tim. 4:10–13). In addition to the biblical record, teamwork has received a large amount of research and promotion in industry and business, so it is reasonable that some churches emphasize team leadership today.

Pastor

Even with the recent emphasis on team leadership, it is still common to find that the senior or solo pastor fills the role of leader. The late parish consultant Lyle Schaller pointed out that the leadership roles of a pastor include being a tribal chief, a medicine man, and an executive officer. As tribal chief, a pastor establishes direction and makes decisions. In the role of a so-called medicine man, the pastor provides care and answers life's big questions. As an executive, the pastor oversees the organization so its goals get accomplished.[1] It's common to hear a church with a strong pastoral leader described as a pastor-led church.

Those who support a single pastor as leader of a congregation often suggest three arguments. First, while leaders in the biblical context (such as Moses, David, and Paul) often embraced teams for support and advice, they usually set direction and made the final decisions. Second, the appointment of elders in every city (Titus 1:5) can be understood to mean single pastors of many smaller house churches. Third, smaller churches historically have been pastored by only one pastor.

Reality

Biblical cases can be, and are, made for each of the above approaches to church leadership. Examples of churches using each of these (and other forms) of leadership can easily be found. It is not my point to argue for or criticize these or any other ways to lead a church. After a half century of both part-time and full-time ministry in various capacities, I've concluded that several different approaches to leadership and church organization can work if (and it's a big *if*) the people are godly and willing to work together.

Let me go further: I've also found that in reality no church will do much of anything that is effective unless the congregation has

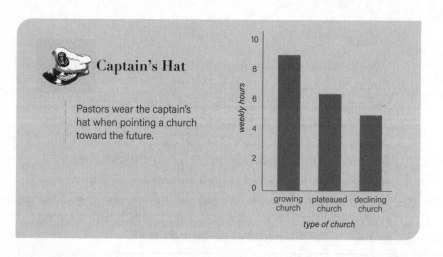

Captain's Hat

Pastors wear the captain's hat when pointing a church toward the future.

confidence that someone is wearing the captain's hat. The person wearing it is usually the pastor, lead elder, or team leader (in this book I'm calling this person the pastor). Pastors of growing churches invest four hours more of their time per week wearing the captain's hat than do pastors of declining churches, and two and a half hours more time per week than pastors of plateaued churches.

The Case of the Missed Opportunity. A Baptist church (name withheld to protect the innocent, or in this case, the guilty) in the suburbs of Seattle, Washington, missed a fabulous opportunity. The pastor called the board's attention to the reality that the area was growing quickly, challenging them to take the bold step of selling the church's old property to relocate to the growing edge of the town. With no further direction (he didn't want to appear dictatorial), and after limited discussion and study of the church's financial situation, the board decided to stay where they were, resulting in the further inward focus of an already underwhelming ministry. A few months later, another church moved to the growing edge of town, quickly becoming the church in the area to attend. This classic story reveals the importance of someone wearing the captain's hat well. What the board should have studied was the opportunity of the situation, but they didn't know how to follow the pastor's visionary lead. The pastor had not given proper leadership. His challenge without further direction was ineffective.

The Case of the Disappearing Pastor. The small Midwestern church was closing, but it had one ministry—a Christian elementary school—that was thriving. The remaining leaders were ready to give their school to another church that would continue to operate it well. After looking at all the nearby churches, they contacted the Presbyterian church to discuss the possibility of them taking over the school. Everything looked good, but there was one problem. The pastor of the Presbyterian church was not available. He was an able man, but his interests were not with his church. As an avid artist, he had turned his garage into an art studio, where he normally spent three days a week sculpting. He lacked the interest in leading his church into the future and seemed to disappear when requests to meet with the leaders of the Christian school came. After repeated attempts to schedule an appointment with the pastor, the leaders of the Christian school decided they couldn't trust him to lead the school well. They decided to turn to another church in town that eventually took over the school. The artistic pastor of the Presbyterian church eventually left to pursue his personal interests in sculpting.

The Case of the Eternal Board. A number of years ago, a church elder board of an independent church in Phoenix, Arizona, sought to develop a long-range plan. They hired one of the top church-consulting firms in America to help them. Following a year of working with the board to establish a planning process, the consultant stepped aside to allow the board to complete the process. Seven years later, the consultant called the board chairperson to check on their progress. He was told, "We haven't finished the plan, but we're having wonderful fellowship." Would the long-range planning process have worked if the board had followed it? I have no idea, but a worshiper told the consultant at the time, "Our board can't make a decision, and the pastor doesn't want to get involved."

In all of these cases, the pastors abdicated their role. The churches lost their momentum, opportunity, and future because the pastor wasn't wearing the captain's hat well.

Wearing the Captain's Hat

When a pastor wears the captain's hat, they are responsible for four major actions.

1. Define the Church's Purpose, Direction, and Meaning

Nothing is more crucial today in many churches. It's common knowledge that people no longer come to church because they must or because of tradition or because of expectations. Simply too many worthy and interesting activities are available to draw them away from church. Think about it. Would you attend a church (or any organization) that didn't know what it stood for or where it was going? Let me get personal. Would you attend your church if you weren't the pastor?[2] People only attend churches that have a clear sense of purpose, direction, and meaning. It's the pastor's job to put on the captain's hat and define the overall purpose, direction, and meaning of the church for people.

Define Purpose

Howard Hendricks from Dallas Seminary used to say, "More failures in the church come about because of an ambiguity of purpose than for any other reason." He's right. Any person or leadership group may plan, dream, and envision the future, but ultimately, it is the Lord's purpose that will stand. It's crucial, therefore, for a pastor to understand God's purpose, clearly communicate it, and help a church pursue it. Why? Because we have God's assurance that it will endure.

In simple terms, the purpose or mission of a church is the biblical reason for its existence.[3] Thus, a pastor must ask and answer questions like, "Why are we (church, believers, etc.) here?" "Why has God left his church on earth?" "What has God commanded us to do?" God, being God, has more than one purpose or mission that he is seeking to accomplish on earth, but it's important to be specific, clear, and simple when defining a church's biblical purpose. Otherwise, a congregation moves about in confusion as to what the church's purpose is. Multiple answers to the above questions are regularly noted, for example, evangelism, worship, education, fellowship, ministry, mission, edification, witness, care, and others. Unfortunately, defining too many purposes for a church is not helpful. Remember: the probability of *not* accomplishing God's purpose for a church increases with the number of purposes communicated. One church I know of spent a year determining its purpose. When the pastor presented it to the congregation, it had fifteen points in all! Net result? No one could remember it, let alone accomplish it. My advice: keep your purpose statement to about fifteen words. (Okay, I'll give you a few more words, but keep it under twenty.) Here's one positive example: "Faithful Church exists to glorify God by making disciples of all people until Christ returns." A lot is packed into that purpose statement—a simply profound, simple statement. People can remember it. People can accomplish it. That's important.

Define Direction

Another important aspect of wearing the captain's hat is to define direction for the church. Most people think of this as a vision or dream. To put it more correctly, a pastor has to help the church discover and act upon God's vision for their particular congregation. Visions (direction) are usually different for each congregation. Needs are different, ministry opportunities are different, and the potential for extending Christ's church is almost limitless. In my experience, believing that God has given your church a unique opportunity for ministry right where it is located is the foundation upon which the vision begins to form.

A vision or sense of direction explains how a church will carry out its understanding of purpose. For instance, you might believe the purpose of the church is evangelism. Explaining precisely *how* your church will go about evangelizing its community becomes its vision. Building on the example of a church's purpose statement noted above, a vision might be something like the following: "To fulfill our purpose of making disciples, Faithful Church will put a copy of the *Jesus* film in every home in our city within the next five years." This sample gives a church direction on how it will fulfill its purpose of making disciples to glorify God.

While wearing the captain's hat, a pastor asks and answers questions like, "How does God desire to express himself in this community, through this church, at this time?" "What is God already doing in our community?" "How can our church get on board with God in our community?" As a pastor prays asking *the* captain of the church, Jesus Christ, for direction, they will gradually come to an understanding of the direction or vision toward which the church should move. Noted leadership expert Robert Greenleaf stated, "Behind every great achievement is a dreamer of great dreams. Much more than a dream is required to bring it to reality; but the dream must be there first."

Define Meaning

Dionne Warwick sings a song that illustrates people's search for meaning when it asks, "What's it all about, Alfie?" The questions people in our churches ask are more profound than asking about love relationships, of course. Deeper questions of meaning, such as, "What's life all about?" "What's church all about?" "What's ministry all about?" emerge frequently. The person wearing the captain's hat must answer these questions.

These questions are of ultimate value. Defining the purpose of a church answers the question, "What are we to do?" Defining the direction of a church answers the question, "How are we going to do it?" Defining the meaning of a church answers the question, "Why are we doing it?" Answering such questions drives a pastor to a larger understanding of God's ultimate purposes. Wearing the captain's hat gives someone the responsibility to help define and shape an agreed-upon set of values for the church. Pastors should ask and answer questions like, "What is really important?" "What are our church's deep-seated, pervasive beliefs?" "What parameters must guide our decisions and actions?"

People in a church expect their pastor, as well as other staff and leaders, to stand for something. They expect them to be courageous. They expect them to be consistent in how they navigate the waves of change coming against churches as nations embrace ever more secular, even anti-faith values. What leaders say and stand for, of course, must be consistent with the aspirations and values of the total congregation. However, someone must express and interpret the values to the larger body, and that person is the one wearing the captain's hat. If a pastor refuses to wear this hat, there's no shared understanding of what's expected. There's no clear knowledge of how people and ministry will be evaluated. There's no commitment to the standards and bottom line of what's important.

DR. MC SEZ

Defining direction is more about belief and passion than slick slogans. To instill strong passion, regularly talk about what you hope the church will become in the future. Paint a verbal picture of what the church will look like when it becomes all God wants it to be. Invest the dream with honest emotion by telling stories of how people's lives have been changed through the church. Act. Do something to start the church moving in the new direction.

2. Generate and Sustain Trust

While everything rises and falls on leadership, everything about leadership rises and falls on trust.

The Case of the Lying Pastor. For a while, Alex (not his real name) wore the captain's hat well. He guided the church to clearly understand its purpose and formulated a vision that the congregation willingly supported. As the church grew steadily from the original 89 people, it hired full-time assistant pastors of children and youth. All moved along smoothly, and the church peaked at

350 in worship attendance. Then things began to crumble as the pastor was caught in a major lie. Confronted, he admitted his lie to the board, who asked him to admit his sin to the congregation and ask for forgiveness. At the next Sunday's two worship services, Pastor Alex spoke in a subdued voice as he admitted his lie and asked the congregation to forgive him. For the most part, the congregation willingly forgave him, many coming up to him after the service to embrace and tell him so personally. His ability to lead, however, was done. Forgiveness was one thing, but trust was another. The congregation could no longer believe what he told them, and he ended up leaving the church for a new ministry.

Another word for trust is credibility. When a pastor has high credibility, people in the congregation are likely to be involved in ministry, tell others about the church, and feel a sense of morale, commitment, and ownership in the church. If a pastor has low credibility, people in the church are likely to seek another church, talk poorly about the church in private conversations, experience low morale, and lack commitment and ownership of the church.

It's the pastor's job to wear the captain's hat in a trustworthy manner. This requires that you walk your talk, follow through on your commitments, and do your job well.

Live the Purpose, Vision, and Values

People in the church must see their pastor personally engaged and enthusiastic about the purpose, vision, and values that are communicated. They want to know the pastor not only talks about these areas but also practices them.

The Case of the Invisible Pastor. In an effort to encourage the congregation at First Lutheran to welcome guests better, Pastor Kirk preached a six-week series of messages on the topic of "Welcoming the Stranger." Throughout the series, he challenged the people to move out of their comfort zones to engage newcomers. A large number of people took up his challenge, but one Sunday, several individuals observed the pastor blatantly ignoring some new attenders. From that point on, most stopped welcoming newcomers and went back to their old ways. One parishioner noted, "If the pastor doesn't really believe what he says, why should I?" Remember: example is not the main thing in influencing others. It is the only thing.

Whatever you determine is the church's purpose, vision, and values, make sure that you are actually living them out, since that is what people want to see. In smaller churches where everyone can observe the pastor's behavior, a lack of living out the church's key mission becomes quickly evident. Pastors in larger churches are not so much in view of the people, yet those around them will see the reality of their commitments. Gradually, the word leaks out that the pastor does not live what they say. It's a classic case of walking your talk. Trust is developed more by what you do than by what you say.

Do What You Say You Will Do

Congregations do not expect perfection. In fact, people want to see some of their pastor's imperfections. It's called authenticity. Nevertheless, people cannot adjust to uncertainty in their leaders. If you say you will do something, and then do not follow through, people will doubt your trustworthiness. So, if you are going to make bold statements about the future and the way you're going to act, be sure you can do what you say. Lack of perfection is one thing; lack of trust is another.

The Case of the Unfulfilled Promises. Pastor Jerry was energetic—some would say extremely energetic. To him, every empty glass was overflowing with possibilities, and he said so. On numerous occasions, he made big promises from the pulpit. At first, the congregation excitedly bought into his dreams, but gradually, they realized that he never followed through on his words. In time, his ability to lead the church dissipated, as people came to ignore what he said.

When you have made a statement or commitment and then discover that it's beyond your ability, it is best to admit it. State directly that the commitment was made too soon, or that circumstances have changed, or that the timing was wrong. In the long run, it is better to be known for making an honest mistake than to be known as someone who cannot be trusted. By being up front with people, you are teaching them that you can be trusted, which will go a long way in gaining their support in the future. Remember: the greatest mistake is trying to always be right.

Demonstrate Knowledge and Skill

When people travel on a common public carrier, such as a train, plane, or ship, it is expected that the person in charge has the knowledge and skill to get them safely to their destination. Similarly, people in churches expect that the pastor has the appropriate knowledge and skill to lead the church. To believe in and get involved in the purpose, vision, and values of the church, people must believe that the person wearing the captain's hat is competent and effective.

The Case of the Unknowledgeable Pastor. Orchard Church struggled for its first five years but somehow managed to survive. At a board meeting, one of the deacons remarked, "What we need is a real vision—a compelling, passionate direction." At that comment, all eyes turned to look at Pastor Foster as if to ask, "Well? What is our vision?" Feeling the questioning glare of his board members, the pastor muttered, "I'm not a visionary person. All I was ever taught in school was to love people and preach the Word."

Demonstrating knowledge and skill does not mean a pastor has to know everything. It does mean a pastor has to be willing to learn what it takes to lead a church. One of the hats a pastor wears is the student's hat (see chapter 7), but it's important to note that a pastor must be able to evoke confidence that they have the skills to lead the church. Otherwise, people will lose confidence in their leadership.

DR. MC SEZ

If you want people to trust you, give it back to them. Too many leaders expect the trust of their people but aren't prepared to give it back. When you give people assignments, tell them what you'd like done, then trust them to figure out how to do it. Ask for advice and then listen carefully to what others say. Take notice of other people's contributions and thank them for their sacrifice and work for Christ and his church. Having trust in your people builds their own confidence to do their best, *and* it stimulates them to trust you in return.

3. Promote Optimism and Hope

Times of transition demand leaders who can inspire and sustain hope. People wonder what the future holds, and someone must wear the captain's hat and inspire hope by promoting visionary possibilities. Promoting optimism and hope means a pastor must be biased toward the future, enthusiastic about the cause, and inspirational.

Biased toward the Future

When it comes to wearing the captain's hat, credibility is perhaps the most important aspect of leadership. Credibility alone, however, is not enough. Congregations expect more from their pastors. People desire their pastor to articulate the exciting possibilities for the future. Thus, pastors must have a bias. They must be biased in seeing the future as better, possible, and desirable. This is directly related to defining the purpose, vision, and values of the church. Even in the midst of struggles, the one wearing the captain's hat points the way to the destination. More importantly, the pastor keeps the morale high by showing how the destination is reachable. It's expected that a pastor be able to look ahead and anticipate the future.

Enthusiastic about the Cause

Making promises that you cannot deliver is a mistake. It's also a mistake to not demonstrate passion for the future of the church. If the pastor doesn't show passion for the future of the church, why should anyone else? People take their cue from the pastor's attitude, voice, and emotions delivered through the sermons and other speaking events large and small. Such passion must be real, honest, and deeply believed. Some pastors try to cover up their real discouragement with happy talk, but people readily see through it. Wearing the captain's hat means that a pastor must have honest hope for the future of the church . . . hope that is built on the solid belief that the purposes of God will be fulfilled.

Inspirational

General George Marshall spoke of the importance of inspiring others: "Morale is the state of mind. It is steadfastness and courage and hope." People in churches desire their pastors to be inspiring, enthusiastic, energetic, and yes, even a bit of a cheerleader. Wearing the captain's hat means being able to inspire and communicate a shared direction (vision) of the future. Of course, pastors have different personalities, and not everyone is a rah-rah type of leader. All effective pastors do, however, have an ability to inspire hope for the future, to raise morale, and to see possibilities.

4. Convert Purpose, Trust, and Hope into Action and Results

An old Chinese proverb asserts, "He who deliberates fully before taking a step will spend his entire life on one leg." The first three aspects of wearing the captain's hat are foundational. A church will not go forward without them. They must be converted, though, into actionable activities that create results. The existence of churches that sport beautiful purpose, vision, and value statements, that trust their pastor, that hope for their futures, but that don't accomplish much is almost commonplace. These are the skeletal aspects, but more needs to be in place to see results. These three elements must be put into action through ministry programs, people's activities, budget alignment, and time allotments. It's the rubber meets the road aspect of reality. Beautiful statements of purpose, vision, and values mean nothing if not put into action in real, tangible ways.

The Captain's Table

No one is capable of leading a church alone. Even though it's important that someone wears the captain's hat, it's equally important to have others sit at the captain's table to offer advice, suggest ideas, ask questions, carry on in prayer, and add skills. Every captain of a ship has a crew comprised of officers, cooks, deckhands, and engineers. They all, at one time or another, in one way or another, contribute to the captain's understanding of running the ship. In the end, though, the captain must wear the captain's hat. Pastors must make decisions, set direction, maintain morale, and perform a host of other actions with confidence in their abilities.

Pastors wear the captain's hat when pointing the church in the right direction. Casting vision for the future cannot be delegated to any other person. Others are invited to sit at the captain's table to give input and advice, but the captain's hat is the second one on the rack and is the basic item in the pastor's apparel.

For Further Reading

Classic: James M. Kouzes and Barry Z. Posner. *The Leadership Challenge*. San Francisco: Jossey-Bass, 1997.

Newer: Warren G. Bennis and Burt Nanus. *Leaders: Strategies for Taking Charge*. New York: Harper Business, 2007.

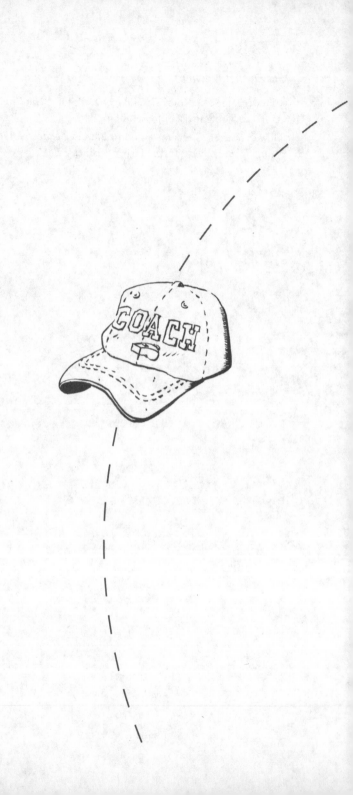

3

The Coach's Hat

Take a moment and think about the people who've helped you in your career or life or family. When I consider the people God has brought into my life, I remember those who pushed me to become better, inspired me to work harder, and challenged me to be the best person possible. One of those people was my junior varsity basketball coach during my sophomore year of high school. He was also my science teacher, and he didn't let me slide by in either place. His challenge to be better spilled over from the basketball court to the classroom, and vice versa. At the time, it wasn't enjoyable. I couldn't get away from his watchful eye and constant pressure to improve. He mandated progress; he was right to do it. My grades improved, as did my play. As a coach, he pushed me to succeed and create a winning attitude, and he made me believe in myself. He instilled a desire to win—yes, win—not at all costs, but to face life with a winning attitude. Even though I never cracked the starting basketball lineup, the lessons he taught have stayed with me for a lifetime. Coaches simply make us better, and one of our goals as pastors is to do the same for others by putting on the coach's hat.

The Case of the Olympic Champion. The name Frank Shorter is legendary in the long-distance running community in the United States (and some places around the world too). He is the only man from the United States to win multiple medals in the Olympic marathon—a gold in Munich in 1972 and a silver in Montreal in 1976. With no coach, he relied on his own determination and will to train. At the Munich games, he boldly took the lead at the nine-mile mark and finished in 2:12:19.8—over two minutes ahead of his nearest competition. His grit and resolve to train without a coach is historic but not recommended. One ingredient found among winners in nearly every field is that *they have a coach.* Professional golfers have swing coaches, business executives have life coaches, singers have voice coaches, and those out of work have career coaches. You name the field, and there is likely a coach to help you improve.

What Do Successful Coaches Do?

The coach's hat is the third one on the rack for pastors. As a coach, the pastor is responsible to get others to play the game as well as

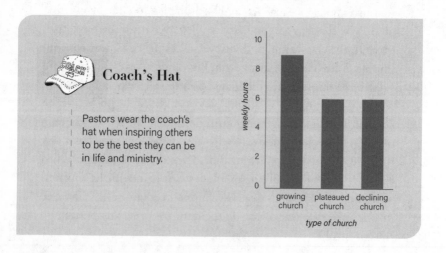

Coach's Hat

Pastors wear the coach's hat when inspiring others to be the best they can be in life and ministry.

possible. When wearing the coach's hat, a pastor observes, corrects, explains, questions, encourages, and inspires others to be the best they can be in life and ministry. Pastors leading growing churches put in 50 percent more time wearing the coach's hat than do pastors in plateaued or declining churches.

What do successful coaches do? The most successful focus on four areas: recruiting, training, coordinating, and motivating.

Recruit

Coaches are always looking for new players—especially A-level players. Such players in church ministry are as rare as they are in sports. Take NBA basketball, for example. There are only a few Kobes, Jordans, or Birds, but lots of Morrisons, Perdues, and Sichtings. You likely have heard of the first three, but unless you're a diehard NBA fan, you probably are unfamiliar with the other three players. The first group are A-level players, while the second group are B-level players. Yet, the teams represented by all of these players would not have won the NBA championship without the B-level players.

Winning teams tend to have at least one star player, but they have many solid mid-level players. The backbone of all churches is not the star players but the mid-level workers who show up and serve week after week. When you wear the coach's hat, stop looking just for the A-level people and recruit more B-level players.

The Case of the Reluctant Cab Driver. Phil and his family had been attending Christ's Lutheran church for over a year. As faithful church attenders, they were quiet spectators, filling the seats like so many others. Phil was reserved. He would not volunteer for anything, even though he desired to serve the church in some capacity.

One evening, Pastor Hunter, always on the lookout for new people to serve, found himself sitting next to Phil at a small group dinner. As the two of them talked, he discovered Phil was interested in accounting (he loved working with facts, figures, and numbers in general). He also learned that Phil felt that no one ever took his interest seriously, because he was, as he put it, "just a cab driver." Pastor Hunter left the dinner impressed with Phil's humble attitude and decided to invite him to work with the church's financial team.

As Phil served on the financial team during the following two years, his talents and spiritual gifts slowly emerged. His personal confidence increased, and people around him expressed appreciation for the excellent work he did on behalf of the church. Today, Phil is a different person. No longer a spectator, he is the church's treasurer. He's a B-level player, but the team would be less effective without him.

At its core, recruitment is discipleship. Christ's final command was to "make disciples" (Matt. 28:19). The command began, however, with an invitation! Christ chose his disciples (Mark 3:13–19; Luke 6:13) and invited (recruited) them (Matt. 4:19). The first requirement when wearing the coach's hat is recruitment.

DR. MC SEZ

The comment heard around many churches is, "We don't have enough people to serve." Such a comment is both true and false. It's true because churches need more workers; it's false because every believer is invested with a spiritual gift and is called upon to serve (1 Pet. 4:10). Like the "Case of the Reluctant Cab Driver," there are numerous people who could serve but must be recruited. Are you recruiting people? Maybe you could improve your own recruitment techniques by using some of the following ideas.

- **Look at every person as a potential team member.** Have you noticed that some people are always finding a good deal on a product, while others never seem to find one? The difference is those who find good deals are looking for them! The same is true for discovering new talent in a church. If you constantly look for new servants, you'll find them. So, keep looking, and don't look away if they're simply a cab driver. Diamonds are regularly found where they are least expected.

- **Encourage people to serve the Lord on the basis of their love for him (2 Cor. 5:14).** Don't ask them to serve as a favor to you, or because the church needs them, or because it won't take much time, or for any number of other reasons. Focus your request on a person's commitment and love for God.

- **Don't downplay the role; magnify it.** This is perhaps the biggest mistake pastors make when recruiting others—downplaying the job. This is seen in the words pastors regularly use when recruiting. Have you heard any of these? "It really won't take much time." "We really don't expect much work." "Can you just do it temporarily until we can find someone else?" Statements like these minimize the role and promote mediocrity. I mean, who wants to do a job that's not important? Look, if the Lord's work is important, we must treat it that way.

- **Don't recruit in the hallway.** If we want to magnify the role, we need to recruit in a way that implies its importance. That means not recruiting as we pass by a person in the lobby or hallway. Rather, make an appointment to sit down with the person and carefully explain the task, clarify what it entails, and detail its importance to the ministry of the church. Tell the individual the bad side of the opportunity as well as the good side. Don't oversell the position. Give people an opportunity to ask questions, and then provide honest answers. Stress the spiritual opportunities of the task.

- **Introduce potential recruits to those already in the same ministry.** If possible, have them shadow others to see what really happens when serving. The dedication and passion of others will make the role more attractive. We all like to work within ministries that have strong personal and social ties. Remember: the more people know about a ministry and those they might be serving with, the more likely they'll say yes.

- **Never expect an immediate answer.** Tell people to take time to think and pray about the opportunity. Let them know you'll be praying along with them. Then give them a date when you'll get back in touch to see what they decide.

Train

Once a person is recruited, they have a right to be trained. All arenas of work or service offer some form of training to their people. Doctors do internships, soldiers go through boot camp, artists apprentice to experts, and athletes are conditioned in training camps. Regrettably, those recruited for Christian service are regularly tossed into the work with little to no training. It's sink or swim, do or die! Why? Why do we neglect training when it comes to Christian service? Many reasons come to mind—lack of time, misplaced priorities, and low value given to the task, to name a few. The largest problem is that we just haven't given it any thought. Quite a few of us in Christian service were recruited and put into ministry with minimal training. We are just perpetuating what we've experienced. Since we made it, we assume others will too. Some do make it, but that's a poor way to train new recruits.

When Christ recruited his disciples ("Follow me"), he also committed himself to them ("I will make you fishers of men") (Matt. 4:19). Note, if you expect people to respond positively to your recruitment, you have to commit yourself to train them. See if the following ideas will help.

First, teach them. An aspect of making disciples is "teaching them to observe all I commanded you" (Matt. 28:20). One only has to read the four Gospels to see that Jesus continually taught his disciples. Instructing new recruits in your beliefs, values, and policies is foundational, but it doesn't end there. The major problem of training people in churches is not telling them what to do but showing them how to do it.

Second, show them. Jesus not only told his disciples what to do, but he also showed them how to do it. Note one example: Christ instructed his disciples, "This is My commandment, that you love one another, just as I have loved you. Greater love has no one than this, that one lay down his life for his friends" (John 15:12–13), and then *he gave his life for them*. There is no substitute for demonstration, for personal example.

Third, allow them. There is a need for new recruits to hear, see, and *do*! Consider how you would train people to swim. You might teach them how to move their arms and legs. Then you might get in the water and demonstrate how to do the same. However, they will never learn to swim until they get in the water themselves and try to do what they've heard and seen. The principle? To train people, you must allow them the chance to make mistakes and learn from their mistakes. No one learns to swim without sinking a few times!

DR. MC SEZ

Coaching involves spending time with people, instructing in the right techniques, demonstrating proper procedures, talking about strategies, and providing feedback on their efforts. In a smaller church, you may be the only coach, but you should start building a team of coaches as quickly as possible. In the meanwhile, start using these coaching insights.

- **Focus on the fundamentals.** The best teams, whether in church, athletics, or business, practice fundamentals. Football linemen practice how to block. Firemen practice how to tie ropes. EMTs practice how to give CPR. What are the fundamentals for the various ministry teams in your church? Teach them, demonstrate them, and practice them.

- **Provide feedback on how people are doing.** Most people do better when given feedback on how they are progressing. The best coaches provide real-time feedback. People want to know how they're doing. Without feedback—positive and negative—learning is hampered, and people's motivation diminishes over time.

- **Treat people with kindness and respect, but expect much of them.** When recruits are treated in a friendly, positive, and pleasant manner, they do better. Words like, "You can do it," "I believe in you," and "I knew you'd be okay" encourage better performance. Set expectations high but communicate belief in their potential to do the task.

- **Reward success.** Watch for new recruits doing the right thing well, then recognize them quickly. Rewards are most effective when given for specific behavior and close to the time of the behavior. Think of the behavior you hope to see and recognize it publicly when it happens. For example, at a team meeting, say, "Sally is being given the Barnabas award this month because she was seen last week helping a family carrying several small children into our building."

- **Hold team meetings.** Gather people from different ministry areas together to analyze the results of their combined efforts. Ask, "Where did we do well?" "What can we improve?" "How can we do things better next week?" Working together on improvement helps everyone involved to improve individually.

Coordinate

Except in a few rare cases, coaches do not play in the game. Their role is to place players where they best fit, where they'll do the best for the team, and where they'll give the team the best chance of winning.

A number of years ago, I was coaching a youth soccer team. My older son showed interest in coaching, and I invited him to coach with me. As it turned out, he was a better coach than I was. We did poorly early in the year, and my son kept telling me, "Dad, the kids are in the wrong places." I finally listened to him and allowed him to put the players where he thought they'd be well suited. We started winning. From that time on, he coordinated the game.

Placing people in the right positions is an art. It takes years of coaching experience and much trial and error to see the nuances that cause others to fit onto a team. You have to pick and place team members with great care. Here are some ideas to consider when placing team members into different roles.

First, examine the person's gifts, talents, or skills. Everyone has a mix of abilities and skills, so narrow down your insights to the primary ones that people bring to the table every day.

Second, determine what contribution a person is making (or will make) to the ministry. Be specific. Ask what would happen if this person wasn't here. Where would this person be missed the most? Occasionally, this will be more difficult than one thinks. If a ministry always goes better when a certain person is there, rest assured they are bringing some skill to the ministry even if it can't be determined. Identify what a person brings to the ministry and put them where they can be most fruitful.

Third, separate ability from compatibility. Some people may wow you with their abilities but not fit well on the team. Those who are oriented to work independently are not as helpful as team-oriented people. A team comprised of all A-level people is usually unfruitful, since all wish to be in the lead. Place people on a team in a way that fosters compatibility.

Fourth, don't judge people based on what others are doing. The primary issue is what they are contributing to the team. Ask what will make them better. Do they need training, education, or mentoring? Once you know the answers to these questions, do your best to get them the needed assistance.

Fifth, move people around until you find their best fit on the team. However, if a fit cannot be found, it's time to consider moving them to an entirely separate place of service. They need to be either coached up or coached out of the task.

Motivate

Pastors are asked, "What is your greatest obstacle in moving the church forward?" One common answer is motivating others to get involved and be part of the process. The answer for how to motivate others is not simple. Here are some suggestions on how to get things moving in the right direction.

First, help others understand *what* needs to happen and *why* it needs to happen. People need to understand and identify the problem to be solved. After understanding the problem, they will be more motivated to help solve it.

Second, keep in mind that everyone is not called, equipped, or motivated toward the same task. All Christians are expected to bear witness to their faith; not all are gifted evangelists. If you attempt to recruit everyone into a single program of evangelism, you are likely to find major resistance. Don't assume that all people will be interested in every program, ministry, or task. Find a person's passion, and then put them where that passion can be best fulfilled.

Third, work together with others to set goals. An old adage says, "Bad goals are your goals; good goals are my goals." It's true. People are best motivated by their own goals. If people can't be motivated, perhaps they are in the wrong areas of ministry. Try moving them to another area where they may be more passionate.

Fourth, reward excellent performance. In business organizations, when you do your job well, you get promoted, and along the way, you get rewards: increased pay, a personal parking spot, etc. It's different in a church, of course (no special restroom for you), but we need to find a way to highlight the results we seek. Here's a way. When you are in meetings, add the following question: "Who have you seen doing something special this week that's helpful to our ministry?" Then thank them. Handwritten notes are of high value (no one writes such notes anymore, which makes a handwritten note distinct). Give a gift card to a local restaurant, or create an award named for a biblical personality who did a similar good work. For example, try the Barnabas award for encouraging others, the David award for courageous effort, or the Philip award for effectiveness in evangelism. Coaches let others know when they've done ministry well.

Fifth, assign everyone a coach or mentor. In sports, veterans are usually assigned to help the rookies. Being coached by a veteran is a major motivating factor, even in church ministry. Push the idea that everyone is to help everyone else, but especially expect veterans to help new recruits.

Sixth, give people latitude and control over how they do ministry. Several studies have found that a major contributing factor to enhancing people's well-being and sense of satisfaction is providing them more freedom to make their own decisions about work and ministry. If people in ministry can't do much without being told what to do, they lose motivation. Technically, this is known as learned powerlessness, and it demotivates. Thus, to motivate people, grant them the power to determine how their ministry is done. Yes, it's risky, but so is being overly controlling.

There is a monumental difference between motivating people and giving orders to people. Coaches can, and do, give orders. The best coaches, the ones who win most frequently, motivate by inspiring, challenging, modeling, and encouraging those on the team. They know how to build a fire under people without burning them.

DR. MC SEZ

The key to motivation is attitude. An individual's attitude is more important than their ability. Motivating starts during recruitment. When recruiting others, probe for insights like these.

- **Are they self-motivated?** Discover the person behind the person: "Tell me about yourself." Learn as much as you can about them. Get a feel for the person. Are there signs of being self-motivated? Or is there evidence that they must be constantly pushed along?
- **Are they future-oriented?** Motivation is intrinsically anchored. Goal setting and motivation go hand in hand. Ask them to share some of their lifetime goals, medium-range goals (e.g., one to five years), and short-term goals (e.g., for the next month). People with no personal goals are often difficult to motivate extrinsically.

- **Are they gracious?** If they spend a great deal of time putting down former pastors, church people, or coworkers, it's a red flag indicating danger. Such people often are only motivated by the chance to criticize others. This is not the person you want on your ministry team.
- **Are they positive?** Ask them to share a story about how they remained positive in the midst of a difficult situation. Were they able to remain motivated during that time?

Motivation is an inside job. Recruiting and placing self-motivated people is the surest way to success.

Game Changers

When wearing the coach's hat, communication is everything. It's not so much what you say but what the people hear and absorb. When the people are in the right places, are motivated for their roles, and are mentored by a good coach, much good is accomplished. In the best situations, lamentably, things change. What if the team stops responding to your coaching? What if your approach no longer seems to work? What then? You must adapt your style, approach, or strategy. Consider the following game changers.

Think of basketball. Years ago, when there was no three-point basket, coaches discouraged players from shooting long-range shots unless it was near the end of the game. The nature of the old game was to work the ball to the center, who could either take a high-percentage shot or pass to another player cutting closer to the basket. Once the three-point shot was allowed, the game changed. Now the game focuses more on passing inside and out and around the perimeter to find the open three-point shot. Coaches had to adjust to a new game. Those who didn't adjust soon found themselves on the losing end and out of a job.

Sometimes this happens to a pastor. The old church game called for home visitation. One successful pastor I knew often said, "A home-going pastor makes a churchgoing people." While that used to be true, few people today desire a home visit from the pastor, particularly if it's unannounced. Church ministry has changed and is changing. Wearing the coach's hat requires constant study and adaptation.

The church has changed. What may have worked when the church was smaller often doesn't work as the church grows larger. Church growth doesn't simply make a church bigger; it makes it different. Leadership style, board responsibilities, staff functions, personal relationships, and ministry roles all change dramatically as a church grows larger. If a pastor doesn't adapt, an artificial ceiling is imposed on the growth of the church. Leaders have to either embrace or resist the necessary changes; so must the congregation.

The people have changed. Coaches must constantly adapt their approach to people. An excellent coach of a sports team understands their players' strengths and weaknesses, then builds a game plan around the team. Similarly, when wearing the coach's hat, a pastor develops a plan that uses the strengths of the people in the church while minimizing their weaknesses. Sometimes a ministry plan is built with a certain group of people, but in time, the personnel changes. People retire, drop out, pass away, and move. The plan you are left with no longer works with the new team of people. You've got to use the people you have, not the people you used to have or wish you had.

The people are not coachable. A pastor can take a church only as far as the church is willing to go. The writer of Hebrews commanded the people to "obey your leaders and submit to them" (Heb. 13:17). It is a challenging message to pastors and people. It implies that people must be willing to be persuaded—they must be teachable and coachable—while also indicating that leaders must lead in a manner that encourages the people to follow. Thus, when wearing the coach's hat, a pastor must coach in a way that encourages the people to listen and follow, but the people must be coachable too. Occasionally, a coach gets a team that just will not listen. They are not coachable.

The voice is the same. "I've been telling them that for years and years!" That is a comment I have heard numerous times following a consultation with a church. Many times, perhaps most, the suggestions I give to a church are not surprises. In fact, most times the pastor has given the congregation the same advice over and over again. In church circles, this experience is called the prophet-without-honor syndrome. Among consultants, it is referred to as the expert syndrome. The scientific term is the coefficient of familiarity. Whatever name you give to this experience, it means the same. Whenever people become too familiar with a person, they tend to not listen to what that person has to say. Over time, the pastor's voice, ideas, and dreams become all too familiar. As one church member once remarked, "We all know the pastor too well. We don't take him seriously any longer." There comes a time when those you lead are simply too comfortable with your ideas, insights, and words. When this happens, either the pastor must reinvent their coaching style, or a new coach will be needed to regain the ear of the people.

The bag is empty. Years ago, doctors made house calls to visit sick patients. When they arrived at a home, they usually had a small black bag in which they carried basic medical equipment and supplies. When pastors first arrive at a church, they don't have a real black bag like a doctor, but they do have an imaginary black bag. In it is everything they know about ministry. When preaching, they reach in and take out what they know about preaching. When planning, they reach in and take out what they know about planning. When coaching others, they reach in and take out what they know about coaching. Over time, a pastor reaches into the bag and is surprised to discover that nothing is left. When a pastor has done all they know to do, the bag is empty. They must either take further training to expand their capacity to coach or move to another ministry that fits their abilities.

In all of these situations, the game has changed. Wearing the coach's hat means you've got to recruit new players, train them in the necessary skills to be successful, place them in the right positions, and motivate them to perform. You also must constantly study the game, your opponents, and the rules. As the game changes, you must change your game plan. If you don't, you'll find less and less fruitfulness in ministry.

For Further Reading

Classic: Howard and William Hendricks. *As Iron Sharpens Iron: Building Character in a Mentoring Relationship*. Chicago: Moody, 1999.

Newer: Robert E. Logan and Sherilyn Carlton. *Coaching 101: Discover the Power of Coaching*. St. Charles, IL: ChurchSmart, 2003.

4

The Executive's Hat

Every four years in the United States, the presidential campaign
mesmerizes the public. Historians recount the great theater created in seven debates between Abraham Lincoln and Stephen
Douglas in the 1860 election, or the fury between Woodrow Wil-
son, William Howard Taft, and Theodore Roosevelt in the 1912
election. More recently, the first televised presidential debate between John F. Kennedy and Richard M. Nixon in the 1960 election
changed history, as Kennedy won due in part to his wise use of
the new media.

A centerpiece of presidential elections is often the stirring ora-
tion at the conventions. Golden-tongued speakers supported with
teleprompters and other ingenious media tools deliver well-crafted
speeches meant to stir up emotional support for candidates. The
speeches made by the candidates and their supporters revel in
bold statements and imagery—promises of what the candidate
will do when elected.

Those kinds of speeches work well during campaigns but not
after a candidate is elected. What works to get a person elected
doesn't work in the real world of governance. The radiance of

grandiose speeches quickly dims once the candidate is sitting in the Oval Office. Eventually, the new president has to deal with issues as they really are, not just as the president feels they should be. Executives have to plan, organize, staff, direct, and evaluate. In other words, they have to manage!

Executives don't wear distinctive hats today, but they used to be seen wearing a traditional fedora hat. Older pictures even show business executives wearing a fedora hat at baseball games. It represents the responsibility all pastors embrace at one level or another. For most, it is the fourth hat on the rack. If it's worn well, a church moves forward. If not worn well, not much of anything happens.

The Case of the Grandiose Sermon. "Folks, if you are committed to reaching our community for Christ, I want you to get up out of your seats and come forward today." A pastor I know made that statement at the end of his first sermon in January. It was a "State of the Church" sort of sermon, wherein the pastor presented a sincere, passionate plea for his church to reach people in the church's ministry area. To the pastor's surprise, it drew a major response. Over half of the people rose from their seats, walked forward, and gathered in front of the pulpit. Trying to disguise his surprise, the pastor quickly thanked everyone for their commitment, offered a prayer of dedication, and dismissed the congregation. Mentally praising himself for preaching such a powerful sermon, the pastor stepped down from the stage only to be met by a small group of people. "What are we going to do now, Pastor?" Shocked by the question, the pastor muttered some nonsense about getting back to them later with next steps. If he had been truly objective, he might have added, "I really didn't expect anyone to respond, so I didn't think about what to do if someone came forward."

Like most pastors, he was sincere in his desire to reach the community for Christ. His ability to communicate the purpose, vision, and values garnered the attention and commitment of the congregation. The quandary? Nothing ever happened after his sermons.

Increasingly, people ignored his pleas for action. He failed to put on the executive's hat and organize the church in such a way that hands and feet were put to his calls for action. Remember: no plan, no action.

Wearing the Executive's Hat

It's common to hear people declare, "Pastors, we are not managers" or "Brothers and sisters, we are not CEOs." These statements are usually made in a genuine effort to correct the perceived imbalance within churches due to some leaders' uncritical use of business practices. The Bible labels church leaders as elders, overseers, and shepherds far more than it speaks of them as managers, leaders, or administrators. At the core of their role, church leaders are to guard the sheep (Acts 20:28–31). Jesus is the Chief Shepherd of the sheep (1 Pet. 5:4) who provides ultimate protection. Nevertheless, he commands, "Shepherd the flock of God among you" (5:2). The primary idea conveyed is that of pastoral or spiritual *oversight* and protection. Their spiritual oversight, however, is multilayered. Pastors protect the flock from false teachers by

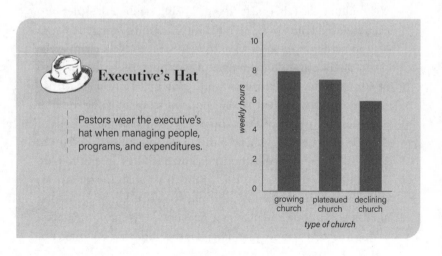

Executive's Hat

Pastors wear the executive's hat when managing people, programs, and expenditures.

preaching and teaching correct doctrine. They protect the flock from selfishness and isolation by focusing on outreach and evangelism. They protect the flock from ineffective and fruitless ministry by organizing and planning. Pastors of growing churches wear the executive's hat two hours more per week than those in declining churches. However, pastors in plateaued churches wear this hat only about half an hour less per week than those in growing churches.

Going Where God Goes

Pastors and others occasionally resist the idea that churches should organize. Their reasons for this vary, but these leaders typically think that management (1) is not needed, (2) is uninteresting, (3) is unbiblical, or (4) lacks trust in God. In response, others point out that a close look at the biblical record demonstrates that God himself is a planner and organizer. He might be called the premier organizer. The principles of organizing and organization are seen throughout Scripture. For example, the early books of the Bible show the nature of God as a planner in creation (Gen. 1), building the ark (Gen. 6), giving the Ten Commandments and law (Exod. 20), building the tabernacle (Exod. 25–30), sending the spies into the promised land (Josh. 2), building Solomon's temple (1 Kings 6), and predicting a succession of kingdoms to Nebuchadnezzar (Dan. 2). The grandest example of planning might be the birth of Christ as the fulfillment of God's plan of salvation (Matt. 1).

God has even created all the good works we're going to do in advance. "For we are His workmanship, created in Christ Jesus to do good works, which God prepared in advance for us to do" (Eph. 2:10). Is James saying pastors and church leaders are not to plan or organize to reach goals? Is it wrong to set goals for tomorrow, next month, or next year? While it may seem that James is speaking against goal setting and planning, he is not. He is speaking against taking a certain pride in planning. It is the pride that is wrong, not the planning itself. Beginning in the first chapter, James presents examples of Christians who take their life into their own hands, with little trust in God.

1:5–8   He warns against double-mindedness.

1:9–11   He warns against dependence on wealth.

1:12–15   He warns against unrepented sin.

1:19–21   He warns against an uncontrolled tongue.

1:22–24   He warns against faith that does not produce fruit.

2:1–13   He warns against showing partiality.

3:13–18   He warns against selfish ambition.

4:1–12   He warns against wrong motives.

It is pride rather than planning that concerns James. He writes, "You ought to say, 'If the Lord wills, we will live and also do this or that.' But, as it is, you boast in your arrogance; all such boasting is evil. Therefore, to one who knows the right thing to do and does not do it, to him it is sin" (4:15–17). James is saying, "Don't take your life into your own hands. Remember that all you do is dependent upon God's will." Christian correspondence from years ago often closed with the letters *DV*, which stand for *Deo volente*, Latin for "if God wills" or "God willing." Planning is not wrong, but all biblical goals are statements of faith. Any statement about tomorrow, next week, or next year is made in faith. Notice how the responsibility of man to plan is balanced with God's will in these verses: "The plans of the heart belong to man, but the answer of the tongue is from the Lord" (Prov. 16:1). "The mind of man plans his way, but the Lord directs his steps" (16:9). "Many plans are in a man's heart, but the counsel of the Lord will stand" (19:21). Faith planning while trusting in God to provide final confirmation and direction is plainly biblical and an action that Christians are expected to practice.

The Case of the Out-of-Tune Horn Player. Lyle was a brand-new Christian when he first went to university. A highly rated high school baritone horn player, he naturally gravitated toward a music career and enrolled in the university's school of music. Toward the end of each semester, all music students were required to perform in front of their teachers. This was mandatory so that the teachers could evaluate their students' growth as musicians. The performance was a major part of each student's semester grade.

As a new Christian, Lyle was drawn to the music of J. S. Bach because at the end of all of his pieces Bach wrote the letters *SDG*, which stands for the Latin *soli Deo gloria* ("For God's glory alone"). At one of the semester recitals, Lyle played a Bach piece and proudly stated, "Bach wrote this for the glory of God, and that's how I want to play the composition."

Disastrously, he went on to present one of the worst performances of his university career and justifiably received a failing grade for it. When Lyle received the paper with his grade, he saw that the professor had written one simple comment: "You can praise the Lord better in tune."

Ministry is done best in tune. If it's the Lord's work and it's worth doing, then it's worth doing well. Don't you agree? Pastors must "exercise oversight" (1 Pet. 5:2), wearing the executive's hat well by planning, organizing, staffing, and evaluating.

Planning

In its simplest form, planning is just deciding what we are going to do in the next few minutes, hours, days, months, or years. Every morning, each of us awakens with some idea of what we're going to do that day. That's planning in the basic form, and we all do it to some degree. From the smallest items (What clothes should we wear today?), to middling issues (Where are we going for vacation next summer?), to major concerns (How much should we save for retirement?), each person makes plans.

DR. MC SEZ

It's easy to talk about the necessity of planning in a church, because the relationship between planning and the stewardship of God's resources is evident. But one thing we don't often talk about is how the relationship between a pastor's personal life and executive life directly impacts their effectiveness. If a pastor doesn't have goals for what they want to be and do in one year, five years, and ten years, how can they expect the church to have such goals?

1. **Purpose.** Effective leaders know their purpose in life. If you have not already done so, write out your life's ultimate purpose in twenty-five words or less.

2. **Dreams.** Effective leaders seek to accomplish a major dream or dreams. If you could be all that God wants you to be and do, what might you accomplish in your life? Write out your dreams.

3. **Goals.** Effective leaders are always working toward several goals. Write out three goals you'd like to reach in the next five years in each of the following areas.

   Career Goals
   Spiritual Goals
   Health Goals
   Family Goals
   Educational Goals
   Financial Goals

Take time to write out your personal goals using the template provided on the next page.

Planning, of course, is both personal and communal. It's as valid for churches as it is for individuals. Still, the average pastor receives little or no training in organizational management before entering pastoral ministry. That's too bad, because as an executive overseer of a church, pastors need such training. It's a shame most have to learn executive skills on their own. Here are some basic planning steps that executives must take.

- Identify key leaders and bring them together.
- Dream about what the church can be in five years.
- Prioritize the best ideas.
- Decide on a few major goals for the next year.
- Align essential people, money, and prayer resources for each goal.
- Write it all down! The weakest ink is sharper than the strongest mind.

My Personal Goals

In the future, I want others to remember me as . . .
(Overall Life Mission in 25 words or less)

Briefly, this Mission Statement means that . . .
(expand on the short statement above in a half page)

In the next five years, I hope to accomplish . . .
(Basic Life Goals)

Career Goals	Spiritual Goals	Health Goals
1.	1.	1.
2.	2.	2.
3.	3.	3.

Family Goals	Educational Goals	Financial Goals
1.	1.	1.
2.	2.	2.
3.	3.	3.

- Communicate your goals in every conceivable manner.
- Meet again in one year to evaluate what happened and set new goals.

Remember: if you're not planning, you're not wearing the executive's hat well.

Organizing

It's quite popular to think that the best organizational structure for a church is to have no structure at all. This is popularly called an *organic structure.* Proponents of an organic structure suggest that a healthy church is one with little or no organization, but this is a crazy idea that misunderstands truly organic structures. Think about the human body. It is organic and natural, while at the same time it's extremely organized (think systems: digestive, circulatory, immune, etc.). Healthy organisms are organized, and that includes a church.

One long-held assumption behind studies of church organization is that *there is one biblically correct form of church.* Of course, what is declared to be the right form of church structure has changed several times throughout history, but that hasn't stopped the search for the one, true form of church structure today. By now, it should be clear that there is no such thing. There is not one biblical way to organize a church; there are many biblical ways. Observation demonstrates that God can and does work through many different organizational structures. He tells us *what* to do (pray, teach, fellowship, worship, preach, witness, plan, etc.) and then leaves the majority of the *how* up to us. By leaving the how open, God allows a church to fit into any cultural context.

Some well-known principles for structuring an organization include the following preferences:

- Simple rather than complex
- Transparent rather than vague
- Flat hierarchy rather than layered structure

- Flexible rather than rigid
- Person-centered rather than program-centered

These principles usually don't tell us how to organize; they tell us what not to do. Leaders have to determine the best way to organize in order to get things done. That's the role of wearing the executive's hat.

The type, style, and approach to organizing depends on the nature of the task. In a crisis, someone must be able to quickly and decisively decide, which requires that someone be in charge (hierarchy). When the church is burning up, executives don't call committee meetings; they give orders. However, when the welcome ministry needs updating, the executives don't give orders. They call together teams of like-minded people to work on changing the system (teamwork). In any church, there is a need for a number of different organizing approaches coexisting side by side.

The work of organizing a church, and the organization that results from this work, is not an absolute but rather a tool for accomplishing God's purpose. Thus, it really doesn't matter how a church organizes to reach its goals, but it does matter that it develops some organizing structure for accomplishing those goals.

Wearing the executive's hat well means a pastor must plan the what, who, where, and when. What is going to be done? Who is going to do it? Where is it going to be done? When is it going to be done?

Staffing

Wearing the executive's hat also means the pastor needs to create an environment for successfully recruiting, training, and developing others, whether volunteers or professionals.

Pastors are not called to do all the ministry themselves, although they often will set the pace. They must oversee the staffing of the church to accomplish its plans. Thinking of professional staff, a pastor puts on the executive's hat by:

- **Hiring the right staff.** The most effective staff have character, competence, and compatibility. They are people of godly, moral makeup, with a Spirit-focused personality. They are able to do the job with excellence and are in sync with the church's culture, purpose, and values.
- **Giving staff members permission to succeed.** Sometimes staff members see themselves as losers. They don't expect more than meager results. The executive's job is to raise their sights to see the opportunities for success.
- **Defining staff expectations.** Staff seldom succeed unless the lead pastor sets clearly defined expectations. Staff share in setting the expectations, but once set, the executive holds them accountable to measurable results. It's not enough to set expectations; follow-up is essential to success.
- **Focusing on staff results.** When staff members make excuses for not accomplishing their goals, they often point out how hard they are working. Effort without results is a great waste. Executives encourage staff to focus on results rather than on the effort of their work. As one executive told a staff member, "Show me the baby; don't tell me about the labor pains."
- **Holding staff accountable.** Executives never put up with mediocre efforts from the staff. They coach them along with questions ("Why did you miss your expectations this year?"), provide resources ("What do you need to succeed next year?"), and call them to account ("Maybe it's best to move on to a place where you can be fruitful").

The Case of the Unproductive Staff Member. "I have a problem." Pastor Williams looked away as he started talking. "One of my staff members isn't accomplishing much. In fact, I'm not sure what he's doing other than preaching at our small Sunday evening service."

His coach, Wayne Summit, quickly interjected, "Let me ask you a couple questions. Have you helped him set any goals for his ministry? If so, when was the last time you met with him to see how he's doing?"

"Well, uh . . ." Pastor Williams hesitated. "Not really. I've never felt comfortable telling my staff what to do or trying to hold them accountable. To tell you the truth, I've avoided asking much about his ministry. I'm afraid of what I might discover."

This story is one that can be observed in numerous churches. Pastors find it difficult to hold staff members accountable for accomplishing goals. Wearing the executive's hat is challenging. How does a pastor hold staff accountable for spiritual work?

DR. MC SEZ

Accountability begins with clearly defined goals. It's part of the necessary work when wearing the executive's hat. I've found the following process works well.

1. **Schedule a private goal-setting meeting with each of your staff members.** Ask them to make a list of what they want to accomplish in the next three months. Talk through their responses to help them narrow down to no more than three key goals. Focus on goals in their primary areas of ministry.

2. **Help them craft their three goals into measurable words.** For example, a statement like, "See my youth group grow spiritually" is not a goal. It's a wish. Ask them what they're actually going to do to help the youth grow spiritually. Force the issue until they arrive at a goal that is specific and measurable. Something like, "I will meet with ten of my young people three times (once a month) for the next three months to train them in how to pray" is a great start.

3. **Ask them what help they need to accomplish each goal.** Do they need training, or money, or extra time, or what? Do your best to provide reasonable resources to make them fruitful.

4. **Pray with them for their ministry, particularly for their success in reaching their goals.** Then, before you end the meeting, schedule another meeting with them to take place four months away.

5. **When the fourth month arrives, meet and ask them how they are doing on reaching their goals.** Did they select ten young people? Did they meet as planned? What did they teach? Ask for copies of materials, outlines, etc. What can they show as results? Go through each goal. Don't let them spiritualize the results but ask for and expect concrete answers. If their goals were met, congratulate them. If not, probe for reasons why. Did they have problems recruiting students to participate? Did they procrastinate? Did they forget? Talk specifically about what went right and wrong. Then, either write out three new goals or reformulate old ones for the next three months. Schedule another meeting in four months and repeat the process.

6. **At the end of a year, you will likely see one of three things.** First, you may discover the staff member effectively set goals and accomplished them. Second, you may find the staff member continually failed to reach their goals. Third, you may find the staff member is somewhere in between. In the first case, rejoice! You've got a winner. In the second case, it's time for a come-to-Jesus meeting—that is, it's time to talk about the staff person moving on to a different position. Is there a better fit in your church for this individual, or is it time for them to move to another church? In the third case, a thorough discussion about the staff person's gifts, abilities, and skills is necessary to determine what they need to be successful (assistance, training, etc.).

This is a simple way to get started. All staff members set three goals every three months and are held accountable for accomplishing their own goals. It's not the pastor telling them what their goals are but guiding them to set their own goals and requiring they work to meet them.

Evaluating

Rabbits tend to jump around a lot, nibbling here, eating there, then running ten feet away and starting over again. Rabbits do that all day. What do they accomplish? It's difficult to say. They do get pretty fat, though.

Churches sometimes fall prey to what Gary M. Gray, former director of the National Institute on Church Management, calls the *rabbit syndrome*. They move toward one goal, then forget it and move in a different direction. On and on, year after year, the church hops from one thing to another, never really accomplishing much at all. They do stay pretty busy, though.

Churches seeking to be faithful to their purpose, vision, and goals must avoid the rabbit syndrome at all costs. One way to do this is to stay focused through evaluation. Every faith plan encounters barriers to its implementation. When congregations encounter blockages to their goals, they often react with doubt (*Was this the right thing to do?*), debate (*Maybe God doesn't want us to go this direction*), or delay (*Let's hold off until we get more clarity*). God uses barriers to test our faith (1 Pet. 1:7) and help us grow personally (Heb. 5:8; James 1:2–4). Evaluation leads us to identify barriers—real versus supposed causes—and seek creative solutions—real versus symptomatic solutions.

Whatever model of planning you use, when wearing the executive's hat, you must formulate a set of criteria for evaluation. Among other items, this includes measurable expectations, specific milestones to determine progress, articulated expectations, and agreement on what is successful, effective, or fruitful.

DR. MC SEZ

Imagine visiting a corn maze in the fall of the year. At one point, you spot a nicely cut doorway leading into the maze. Your curiosity draws you into the passageway, and you follow it around, right and left, left and right. Then suddenly, it dawns on you that you are in a labyrinth. Later, as the puzzle settles in, you realize you are lost.

Mazes are infinitely more tractable when viewed from above. If you could look down on the labyrinth from, say, a perch high up in a tree, your eye could take in the whole of the maze—the starting door, the passageways, the turns, and the walls—and solutions would be revealed immediately.

Wearing the executive's hat is much the same. It is seeking to look down on the various directions that the church might go in the future and predetermining a course of action—not in pride as if leaving God out but in humility believing God has already planned the way.

Lessons in Wearing the Executive's Hat

Here are some practical lessons for wearing the executive's hat well. Each lesson is related to the next. Like with Russian nesting dolls, you'll open up one and find there's another one inside.

First, pastors who wear the executive's hat well have the following character qualities:

- **Curious.** They ask questions, probe back stories, wonder how they can make things better. They love a challenge that takes them out of their comfort zones.
- **Humble.** They know what they don't know and are okay with it. They draw people around them who know more about things than they do and trust them to speak truth.
- **Decisive.** They believe that a little chaos leads to creativity and have confidence to make decisions amid ambiguity.
- **Empathetic.** They care about people but are willing to let them go if they are impeding the ministry.
- **Patient.** They understand that change often happens slowly but create a sense of urgency for the future.

Second, effective executives get out of the office. They walk around, ask questions, observe what is actually happening, and talk to volunteers. They make sure that people in all ministry areas are heading in the same direction as those in the top leadership positions.

Third, pastors who wear the executive's hat understand you can't avoid Murphy's Law. If anything can go wrong, it will. They live with one foot in reality and the other foot solidly in the plan. A lot of plans that look good on paper don't work in the day-to-day life of the church. Wearing the executive's hat requires facing reality.

Fourth, pastors who wear the executive's hat don't wait to do something until everything is perfect. They plan, set goals, recruit staff, get going, evaluate, and make corrections on the go. Nothing gets done if you wait until it looks perfect.

Fifth, pastors who wear the executive's hat realize they won't bat a thousand. A baseball player who makes an out 65 percent of the time bats .350 and is likely to win the batting championship! You will be a champion executive even if every plan or goal doesn't succeed.

Sixth, pastors who wear the executive's hat follow through on their plans. A pastor can't simply make decisions; they must also follow through. Doing so requires a closed-loop system to make sure that decisions are executed. The basic concept is that the one wearing the executive's hat must receive continuous feedback to learn how the plans are being fulfilled. Plans are put into action, feedback on results is received, and adjustments are incorporated into the plans, which are then placed into action again. Whatever system an executive devises, it's certain that no decision means much until it is accomplished.

Seventh, anyone wearing the executive's hat relies on staff expertise, survey data, suggestions from outside consultants, and other forms of helpful information and advice. At some point, the executive must perform an act of faith in deciding what the church will actually do. While putting ultimate trust in the Lord for the faith plan, the executive must take responsibility. This requires emotional, psychological, and spiritual strength. As a pastor, you may already have this strength to some degree, but extra work through classes, books, and mentors will aid your growth.

With their constant time-consuming responsibilities, pastors may find the executive's hat a challenging one to wear. It is, however, the one that makes things happen on the ground. It is the fourth-most-important hat to wear to help your church grow.

For Further Reading

Classic: Ted W. Engstrom and Edward R. Dayton. *The Art of Management for Christian Leaders.* Waco: Word Books, 1976.

Newer: Michael J. Anthony and James Estep Jr., eds. *Management Essentials for Christian Ministries.* Nashville: B&H, 2005.

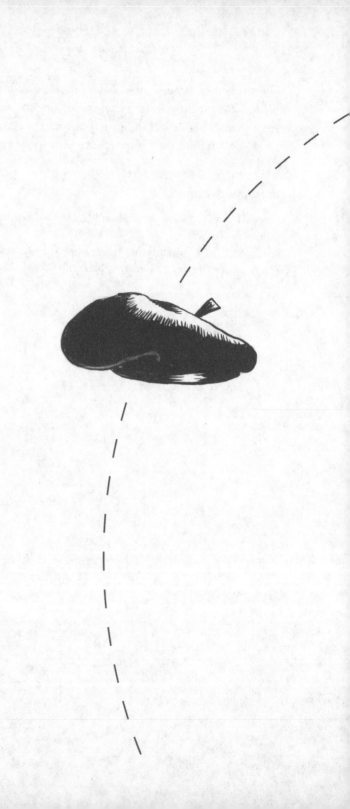

5

The Director's Hat

Have you seen one of those movies or television shows that takes place on a movie set? Do you remember the person who sits in a canvas chair with "DIRECTOR" printed in large letters on the back? As directors work with actors to film a story, they shout out commands such as "Action!" "Cut!" and "That's a wrap!" The director's role is to direct the actors, photographers, lighting personnel, gaffers, sound engineers, and stuntpeople to perform to the best of their abilities. In old movies, directors often wore a beret, which symbolized their status as impresarios, a word borrowed directly from Italian, which like our English word *emprise* carries the connotation of seizing an adventurous, daring enterprise.

When pastors wear the director's hat, they seize an adventurous, daring enterprise—making disciples of all people! The last words of Jesus to his disciples included a command to "make disciples" (Matt. 28:19). The Greek word translated here as "disciple" is found only in the Gospels and Acts. It does not appear in the Epistles at all. Neither Paul nor Peter used the word, in part because it is a descriptive term, more suitable for biography than for doctrine or exhortation. *Disciple* is synonymous with

Christian, that is, a true believer (Acts 11:26). In general, the word *disciple* describes a person who follows Jesus and learns from him. This includes men and women (Luke 14:26; Acts 9:36) with wide-ranging levels of commitment, from the merely interested to the strongly committed, from the mature to the immature (Matt. 26:56; John 6:66; Acts 6:7; 14:21). Thus, in wearing the director's hat, pastors work to enroll as many people as possible in Christ's school to learn of him. Pastors in growing churches wear the director's hat two hours more per week than those in declining churches while only a half hour more per week than those in plateaued ones.

What's a Disciple?

It is clear that the word *disciple,* as used in the early first century, covers a rather large number of people, even those who were simply curious about Jesus. Yet, as time moved along, Jesus called his followers to move beyond basic curiosity to believe in him. An example of this is found in John 6:66–71. Many of Jesus's disciples (the curious) left him. Immediately, Jesus looked at the

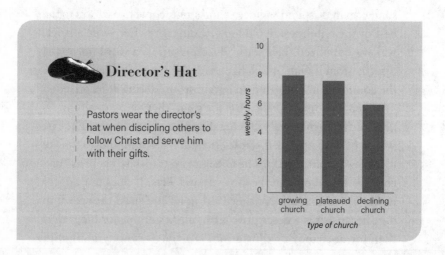

Director's Hat

Pastors wear the director's hat when discipling others to follow Christ and serve him with their gifts.

weekly hours

type of church

growing church plateaued church declining church

twelve disciples and asked, "You do not want to go away also, do you?" (v. 67). Peter replied, "Lord, to whom shall we go? You have the words of eternal life. We have believed and have come to know that You are the Holy One of God" (v. 68). To be a disciple in a technical sense is to truly believe, to pass from curiosity to conviction. From the moment of new birth, all Christians are Christ's disciples.

After the incident in John 6, the word *disciple* is used only of people who profess to believe in Jesus Christ for eternal life. Jesus increasingly called for his disciples to count the cost. He used challenging words and phrases: take up your cross, hate mother and father, sell all you own. It was an all-or-nothing call to remove other priorities—religious, economic, or familial—to make Jesus Savior and Lord. Every true believer is a disciple, but growth into maturity is a process; disciples are always becoming more fully disciples. Thus, a disciple is a person who has received Jesus Christ as Savior and is growing in obedience to him so that they are becoming more like Christ.

Pastors must put on the director's hat and lead the church to live out the command of Christ to make disciples who demonstrate three commitments: commitment to Jesus Christ (John 8:31), commitment to the body of Christ (13:34–35), and commitment to the work of Christ in the world (15:8).

The Case of the Gifted Evangelist. The pastor of Laurel Woods Friends Church, LeRoy Harris, was what you might call a gifted evangelist. When he arrived at the church, only thirty-four people attended worship services. He had counted sixty-five people who came out to meet him when he preached the first Sunday, but that number soon drifted down to the small group of people who greeted him each Sunday.

Since Pastor Harris was not the type to get discouraged, he got busy walking the Laurel Woods neighborhood, meeting, greeting, and befriending numerous people. He was a natural evangelist, and it wasn't long before new people started showing up on Sunday morning. It was outstanding, even dramatic, but by the end of his second year, Laurel Woods Friends was averaging 315 worshipers on Sunday morning. Every one of the new people looked to the pastor as their spiritual father, which was understandable since he'd led each one to faith in Christ. To most of the new people, he was the only pastor they'd ever known and trusted.

Laurel Woods Friends Church continued to grow, that is, until another Friends church from a nearby town came calling. Their leaders had heard about the fantastic growth at Laurel Woods and wanted to see with their own eyes what was happening. During their visit, they discretely inquired if Pastor Harris might consider becoming the pastor of their church. It just so happened that, toward the end of Pastor Harris's third year at Laurel Woods Friends, he left for a new church. His leaving wouldn't have been all that bad but for the fact that the new members also left. Slowly at first, but at an ever-increasing speed, the worship attendance dropped down to just about the same as it originally was three years before—thirty-five people.

Although the pastor was an effective evangelist, he didn't follow up with the new converts with any solid form of discipleship. The new members were not instructed in the importance of faithful financial giving, the value of participating in small group ministry for fellowship, or the worth of serving in a ministry. The only aspect of discipleship they were taught was that of worship attendance. In the end, it wasn't enough when their beloved father in the faith left for another church.

Disciple Making

The fact that the word *disciple* doesn't appear in the Epistles implies that discipleship takes place organically within the context of the local church. The church is its own discipleship model. It has an internal organization, structure, and climate, which blend together in a supernatural way to develop disciples.

The ministry of the early disciples demonstrates two types of disciple-making processes: public and private. For example, Peter preached *publicly* on the day of Pentecost (Acts 2:14) with the result that some three thousand people decided to follow Christ. A short while later, he spoke *privately* in the home of Cornelius, where many believed in Christ (10:23–24). Philip evangelized *publicly* in Samaria (8:5), then spoke *privately* with an Ethiopian eunuch (8:26). Paul proclaimed Christ *publicly* in Damascus (9:20) and sometime later dealt *privately* with Timothy (16:1–2). Jesus modeled the same rhythm of public and private ministry. He spoke *publicly* to masses of people (Matt. 14:13–21; 15:29–38). Yet, he engaged in intense *private* teaching and training of his small group of disciples (16:13–28; 17:13).

The rhythm of disciple making flows back and forth between these two dynamics—public and private—in the life of a church. Allow me to offer two definitions. *Public discipleship* is the process of spiritual growth that takes place in all believers as they are exposed to, and involved in, the life of a local church. *Private discipleship* is the intense concentration of attention on a person or small group of people for the purpose of leadership development. They look like the following:

Public versus Private Discipleship

Public Discipleship	Private Discipleship
Focus is on the many.	Focus is on the few.
Emphasis is one-to-many.	Emphasis is one-to-one.
Purpose is to develop the body.	Purpose is to develop leaders.
Method is body life together.	Method is individual training.
Demonstrated in the Epistles.	Demonstrated in Gospels/Acts.

Public Discipleship

God has initiated processes in a local church, which result in the discipling of its members. An overview of this idea, but not an exact process, is presented in Ephesians 4:11–16. In this well-known passage of Scripture, Paul explained that Christ gave leaders—apostles, prophets, evangelists, pastors, and teachers—for the "equipping of the saints" (v. 12). The Greek word translated as "equip" is a rare word that means "to mend." It's used to refer to the repairing of a fishing net so that it can be used to catch fish again (Matt. 4:21). Another image is of a physician setting a broken bone or dislocated joint. The essential idea is that leaders are to restore broken people so that they are useful to the Lord's work. Wearing the director's hat well is to equip (repair, mend) disciples so that they may engage in Christ's work so the church, the body of Christ, is strengthened. This is to continue until every individual in the church is mature—"until we all attain to the unity of the faith, and of the knowledge of the Son of God, to a mature man, to the measure of the stature which belongs to the fullness of Christ" (Eph. 4:13). Stated in a few words, the goal of public discipleship is to help people in your congregation become like Christ (Rom. 8:29). Christ Jesus said it himself: "It is enough for the disciple that he become like his teacher, and the slave like his master" (Matt. 10:25).

Nothing describes public discipleship better than images of *body life*. People are equipped and matured when they live life together. Perhaps that is why we are admonished to stir up one another to love and good works. How do we accomplish that goal? We must not neglect to meet together (Heb. 10:25). It's in the meeting together that discipleship happens as we love (John 13:34–35), encourage (1 Thess. 4:18), exhort (Heb. 3:13), forgive (Col. 3:13), confess and pray (James 5:16), sympathize (1 Pet. 3:8), serve (Gal. 5:13), are patient (Eph. 4:2), are kind (Eph. 4:32), bear one another's burdens (Gal. 6:2), practice humility (1 Pet. 5:5), and work for unity (Eph. 4:3). All these good things happen naturally as people are together, loving and serving each other. It's public disciple making that brings maturity to the body as a whole. What ingredients bring about maturity? It's the basics: biblical preaching/teaching, fellowship, communion, prayer, witness, worship, etc. (Acts 2:42). As people participate in worship, sit under the preaching and teaching of God's Word, engage in prayer, participate in community, give witness to their faith among family and friends, and fellowship together, they grow. Consequently, how do you count? How do you know if you are making disciples in the larger public sense?

How Do You Count?

You may be against counting disciples, feeling that it's not godly to do so. Many pastors are these days. Yet, you no doubt count the offerings and other items of less importance than disciples. The Holy Spirit thought it important to count disciples. Scripture records the calling of 12 apostles, the sending of 70, the gathering of 120 fearful souls, the conversion of 3,000 at Pentecost, and the feeding of 5,000. So why not count disciples too?

During recent church history, most pastors assumed that church attendance was enough to indicate that people were disciples. Even though counting worship attendance is not as attractive as it once was, there are still valid reasons for doing so. It is theologically sound. If you believe proclamation of God's Word and the administration of the sacraments (or ordinances)are crucial aspects of discipleship, you'll have little problem finding theological justification for using worship attendance as an indicator of discipleship. It is a barometer of change. It's much like your blood pressure—it doesn't tell you everything, but it's an important indicator of your health. It is the best single predictor for aspects of church programming, such as financial giving and the need for ministry staff, increased space, and leadership. However, it doesn't tell you if people are becoming mature, i.e., growing into the likeness of Christ. For this reason, you should consider an additional and connected model of counting how well your public discipleship ministry is working.

First, decide on five to seven key indicators that demonstrate your church is effectively making disciples. The most commonly selected indicators are worship attendance, small group attendance, serving in a ministry, financial giving, and number of baptisms (usually meaning adult baptisms or conversions). Feel free to select these or a few more indicators you feel are indicative of your church's disciple-making strength.

Second, rank your indicators on a scale of 1 to 5, with 5 being the most important (if you have five indicators). Use a scale that is the same number as your total indicators. Thus, seven indicators would use a scale from 1 to 7, etc.

Third, create a chart with the major indicators based on your ranking from top to bottom.

Fourth, count the yearly averages or exact numbers, as the indicator warrants, for one year, and enter the numbers into the chart.

Fifth, multiply the yearly numbers with the weighted number of your scale. The result is your *discipleship maturity scale*.

Here's an example using the five indicators mentioned:

DISCIPLESHIP MATURITY SCALE

Indicator	Weighting	Year 1	Year 2
Baptisms	5	×15 = 75	×18 = 90
People serving	4	×37 = 148	×42 =168
Small group attendance	3	×74 = 222	×83 = 249
Financial giving	2	×55 = 110	×65 = 130
Worship attendance	1	×110 = 110	×128 = 128
Total		**665**	**765 (15% increase)**

Using a discipleship maturity scale creates a balanced view of how well your church is making disciples through its public ministries. It doesn't rely on just one or two indicators, but it mixes several important values to give a better understanding of your public discipleship. It fits your church's context and philosophy of ministry because you select the indicators and weight them according to the value you select. It's vital that you carefully think through your own view of ministry, selecting and weighting the indicators accordingly. Once the indicators are selected and weighted, you must keep them in place so that comparisons can be made accurately from year to year. Note in the example how year 2 is compared to year 1. Over a number of years, you'll be able to see if your public discipleship ministry is healthy or unhealthy. Remember: you measure what you value; you value what you measure. If you're wearing the director's hat well, you'll know the score!

DR. MC SEZ

People attribute much of what happens in life to luck or coincidence. As Christians, we don't like to use the language of *luck*, preferring to give credit for success or failure to God's power or providence. It's unlikely, however, that Jesus Christ would have commanded us to make disciples if it couldn't be accomplished. So, it must be possible to do so. While we recognize that God is sovereign and that life does happen within his providence, we need to act with focus, to act deliberately. Someone once commented, "The harder I work, the luckier I get." Similarly, I say, "The more deliberately we focus on making disciples, the more disciples we'll make."

Private Discipleship

The *Peanuts* comic strip is read by millions of people every day. In one *Peanuts* cartoon, Charlie Brown visits Lucy's psychiatry stand and confesses, "Sometimes I think I don't know anything about life. I need help. Tell me a great truth!"

Lucy replies, "Did you ever wake up at night and want a drink of water?"

"Sure," says Charlie, "quite often."

"When you are getting a drink of water in the dark," Lucy goes on, "always rinse out the glass because there might be a bug in it! Five cents, please."

"Great truths," comments Charlie, "are even more simple than I thought they were."[1]

I suggest that they really are. One great truth about disciple making is that *God's method is people.* Jesus's plan to change the world was not complex: "He appointed twelve, so that they would be with Him and that He could send them out" (Mark 3:14). The tendency of pastors—perhaps even you—is to make disciple making difficult. Jesus's approach, though, was profoundly simple: companionship and commission. One invigorates the other. Private discipleship, like raising children, is impossible by proxy. If you desire to build up a team of leaders to accomplish God's purposes in your church, you must spend time with a few people. Jesus's disciples ate with him, talked with him, fished with him, prayed with him, and, in doing so, became like him. Later when people observed the power of the disciples, they recognized that "they had been with Jesus" (Acts 4:13 ESV). It's a scary thought, but in time, people in your church will become like you. You can't stop it from happening any more than you can stop children from becoming like their parents. Paul recognized this and lived it. Three times Paul exhorted his followers to "be imitators of me" (1 Cor. 4:16). "Be imitators of me, just as I also am of Christ" (11:1). "Brethren, join in following my example" (Phil. 3:17).

DR. MC SEZ

"Who are your disciples?" It's a great question, and one you should ask yourself right now. Can you name a person or a few persons whom you are meeting with weekly or monthly? Here are some ideas on how to get started.

1. **Pray about the larger Christian body you are serving.** Ask God to lead you to a few people whom you can develop as leaders (Luke 6:12).

2. **Choose a few people to invest your life in, but don't select too many (Luke 6:13).** Remember, Jesus spent most of his time with only twelve people, and one of them drifted away. Three to ten people are enough with which to start.

3. **Spend time with this group (John 3:22).** As much as possible, involve them in your family, leisure, personal, and ministry life. Offer times for teaching and discussing the Bible together. Encourage them to share their lives with each other, and set the pace by your own openness and vulnerability.

4. **Be aware of teachable moments when your disciples are receptive to learning (Mark 10:13-16).** Welcome challenging events as times for growth (4:35-41).

5. **Convey a vision to disciple others, and send them out to cultivate ministries of their own (John 20:21).** Slowly move your disciples into positions of increased responsibility. Push them into new situations that stretch their faith and skills (Mark 6:7-13). Support them with counseling and encouragement when they are on their own. Provide help as they request it (Matt. 13:10; 17:19; Luke 17:5).

6. **Don't give up.** Making disciples can be disappointing and discouraging at times. Judas betrayed Jesus (Matt. 26:47-50), Peter denied him (26:69-75), and Thomas doubted (John 20:24-25). Later, Peter returned and wrote two epistles, and Thomas confessed the Lord's deity. Your disciples may fail you, but they too may change.

Remember: when it comes to leadership development, *more time spent with fewer people results in larger impact on more people.*

Private discipleship is the intense concentration of attention on a person or small group of people for the purpose of spiritual growth and leadership development. The following principles are essential to understand if we hope to faithfully make disciples.

First, discipleship involves investing in the lives of future generations. When Jesus gathered his band of twelve disciples, he started a chain of multiplication. He discipled Andrew, who reached his brother Peter, who reached some three thousand people on the day of Pentecost (Acts 2:38–41). Barnabas discipled Saul (Paul) and John Mark. Priscilla and Aquila discipled Apollos, and Paul discipled Timothy, Titus, and others.

Second, discipleship involves training a few to reach the many. The purpose of discipleship is not selfish. Rather, it is to train a few people who will ultimately take the gospel of salvation to countless others. Disciples are to be witnesses to Christ's work (Acts 1:8), to go preaching the Word (8:4–14), and to plant churches among all ethnic groups (8:26–40).

Third, discipleship involves a lifestyle that must be developed. Those who are discipled are to develop a lifestyle whereby they teach what they know to others. This is a process that never ends, as we see in 2 Timothy 2:2, where Paul writes, "What you have heard from me in the presence of many witnesses entrust to faithful men, who will be able to teach others also" (ESV).

Fourth, discipleship involves seeing potential in others. A good example is Barnabas, who was the first to see potential in the person of Saul (aka Paul, Acts 9:27). After Saul's conversion, it was Barnabas who encouraged the disciples at Damascus to accept him.

Fifth, discipleship involves selecting people to disciple. When Barnabas was faced with a challenging ministry in Antioch, he immediately "left for Tarsus to look for Saul" (Acts 11:25).

Sixth, discipleship involves sharing ministry with others. After Barnabas found Saul, "he brought him to Antioch. And for an entire year they met with the church and taught considerable numbers" (Acts 11:26). Serving together is the primary way to train disciples. It is the method used by Jesus, Barnabas, and eventually Paul.

Seventh, discipleship involves a change in leadership. This is often the most difficult aspect of discipleship, i.e., letting our disciples lead us. This is seen in the way the names of Barnabas and Paul are placed in the various passages where they are mentioned together. In all places, up through their appointment as missionaries in Acts 13:1–3, the name of Barnabas is always listed before that of Saul (Paul). However, in Acts 13:42–43, the names are switched, with Paul's name placed before Barnabas's name. Most likely, this is an indication that Paul assumed the leadership role. It is worth noting that Barnabas apparently accepted this with no regrets.

Eighth, discipleship involves letting disciples go. Barnabas and Paul eventually went their separate ways in ministry (Acts 15:36–40), which may not be as bad as some have thought, for their ministry was then multiplied.

As you observe the people around you, whom do you think has potential? People who give evidence of potential are usually self-starters who are already committed. They often appear ordinary but are caring and eager to help. Have you asked them to help you in ministry? Discipleship takes place predominately in the doing of ministry together, not in a class. Conversations before, during, and after serving together are the times when disciples are most teachable. When was the last time you met with this potential disciple? It takes time to build the kind of trusting relationship that is necessary to disciple others. Regular times together are important. So, who are you discipling?

If no one, when are you going to get started?

– – – – –

The Case of the Jack-of-All-Trades Pastor. Pastor Lanny Rodgers loved leading his medium-sized neighborhood church in song each Sunday morning. Then too, he enjoyed preaching on Sundays to the crowd of 165 worshipers. Because of his strong people skills, he spent significant time counseling members of the congregation and, as word leaked out, people outside the church as well.

Actually, Pastor Rodgers liked all aspects of ministry, but repeatedly he was heard saying, "I don't understand why more people don't step up and help more." To some in the congregation, this was a quandary, because Pastor Rodgers appeared to want new leaders to step forward, but in practice he wouldn't let anyone else lead.

Take last Sunday morning's worship service as an illustration. Pastor Rodgers walked to the piano, sat down, and as he pulled the microphone close to his mouth, said, "Let's draw near to the Lord in worship." In his previous church, Pastor Rodgers had served seven years as a worship pastor. He had excellent skills at leading worship and felt that to maintain a certain level of excellence, to honor the Lord of course, he was the best person to lead worship at his own church. When the worship set was over, Pastor Rodgers stepped up on the platform and, while opening his Bible, said, "Let's listen to the Word of the Lord." After reading the morning Scripture, he led the congregation in prayer and then called for the ushers to come forward to take the morning offering. Next, he handed the offering bags to the usher and then returned to the piano to play the offertory. At the conclusion of the offertory, he then moved back to the stage and commenced the morning sermon. Then, you no doubt will guess it, when the sermon was completed, he proceeded to play the closing song on the piano and finished the morning with a closing prayer.

As he walked out of the auditorium toward the lobby, a man was overheard commenting under his breath to his wife, "Can't anyone else in this church pray, or play the piano, or take the offering?" His embarrassed wife responded, "Shush!" but the man's analysis was precise. Others *could* pray, play the piano, lead worship, or pray for the offering. Pastor Rodgers was his own worst enemy. His excuse of wanting to do everything with excellence covered his inability to develop leaders.

Developing Leaders

Every Christian leads in some way. They may lead poorly, but they still lead. Since all believers have at least one spiritual gift (see 1 Pet. 4:10–11), they are all under obligation to use their gifts in serving others. So, why do most churches seem to struggle to find leaders? The reasons are numerous, but some of the major ones are as follows.

- Some people feel inadequate, believing others can do a better job.
- Some feel that church work is not important.
- Some find church ministry unattractive or not challenging enough.
- Some feel they are too busy to give time to leading in a church.
- Some experienced failure in a previous attempt at leadership and don't want to take a chance of failing again.
- Some are spiritually indifferent, not aware that God has uniquely gifted them to lead.
- Some have wrong priorities, placing less worthy things ahead of church service.
- Some are just too modest and don't desire to push their way forward.
- Some are burned out from previous leadership experiences.

I've discovered, however, that these are not the main issues. Rather, the three primary reasons people don't get involved in leadership are first, the church has no plan to recruit, train, and involve new people in leadership. Second, they have never been asked personally to get involved. Third, there is no clear pathway into leadership, i.e., people don't know how to get involved. Does your church have a plan and a clear pathway for new people to follow toward leadership? If not, try the following ideas.

Develop a Farm Team

Take a tip from professional baseball and develop a farm team. Start by establishing a file of potential leaders. You can find possible leaders among new worshipers, church guests, those who are inactive, and those who are already serving in support roles. Make a list of all your church attendees and then take everyone who is already involved in leadership off the list. From the list that remains, begin to build a farm team. Give this list to all current leaders, and ask them to find an apprentice from someone on the list. Keep asking them to do this until they do it. By adding one apprentice to every current leadership position, you will build a farm team of potential leaders.

Write Ministry Job Descriptions

Ask the leaders of all church ministries to write ministry job descriptions for each of the positions they oversee. These descriptions should be one page long, written in bullet point style, with the following information: ministry title, monthly time involvement, length of commitment, to whom they report, basic job responsibilities or duties, training available, and expectations and/or requirements. Ministry job descriptions provide people with clarity about what they have been asked to do.

Organize a Ministry Placement Team

Find a person who has some background in human resource management and ask them to organize a ministry placement team. Give this team the responsibility of designing a complete leadership recruitment strategy for the entire church. The plan should include designing a simple pathway into leadership and communicating it to the entire congregation; developing a class to teach people their spiritual gifts; holding personal interviews with all attendees to discover their unique design for ministry; placing them one by one in ministry positions; monitoring those who are placed to make certain each continues in leadership; and helping them find a place to apprentice.

Build a Total Leadership Training Process

Provide a one-year training program for select leaders in your church. Limit involvement to about twelve people a year. Make the training high quality and high commitment. Invest a significant amount of money each year into this program, and be sure to highlight the graduates with a ceremony, special shirts only for graduates, and so forth.

Does your church have a leadership training plan? If not, why not? When will you begin to start one?

Discipleship exists in a rhythm of public and private ministry, a tempo of discipleship that takes place through the natural corporate ministry of a local church and through individual leadership development. If you desire to wear the director's hat, you'll need to balance both of these aspects in the life of your church.

For Further Reading

Classic: Robert Clinton. *The Making of a Leader: Recognizing the Lessons and Stages of Leadership Development*. 2nd ed. Colorado Springs: NavPress, 2012.

Newer: Eric Geiger and Kevin Peck. *Designed to Lead: The Church and Leadership Development*. Nashville: B&H, 2016.

6

The Counselor's Hat

Young children like firefighters. I suppose the fascination is tied to the cool outfit they wear or to the sound of a siren screaming loudly as a bright red fire truck rolls briskly down the street. What child, when watching such a scene, wouldn't want to be riding in the firetruck? I'd personally like to sound the siren. Wouldn't you? Add in the impression that firefighters often are rescuing people or animals in desperate situations, and it's easy to see why children are attracted to them. What children don't see, of course, is the slow pace of life that firefighters live day to day while waiting for the fire bell to ring. Most of their time is spent cooking meals, cleaning the firehouse, repairing equipment, practicing fire drills, or inspecting local businesses for compliance to fire laws—activities that are completed while waiting for the bell to ring.

Wearing the counselor's hat is much like playing firefighter for pastors. They wait through the humdrum of pastoral life—phone calls, meetings, and such stuff—for the bell to ring so they can rush out to rescue someone in distress and be the hero, the one called when life gets desperate. Granted, the counselor's hat isn't always worn in rip-roaring situations. It's often more akin to a camp counselor who cares for campers, nurses small scrapes and bruises, and mediates silly disputes, all in the hope of getting through the week with no major injuries.

The counselor's hat is often the most exhausting to wear. It is worn each time a pastor meets with people seeking help with personal problems and issues. Meetings can be positive (e.g., premarital counseling) or negative (e.g., advising couples seeking divorce). Counseling can be melancholy (e.g., helping people prepare for funerals) or happy (e.g., preparing parents to dedicate a baby to God). Caregiving activities include counseling and advisement on career issues, managing conflict, listening to complaints, and a myriad of other emotionally draining engagements. It's often overwhelming. As any pastor knows, there are eternal ramifications when wearing the counselor's hat, and there is no end to people's needs. Pastors in growing churches wear the counselor's hat two hours more per week than those in declining churches but just a half hour more per week than those in plateaued churches.

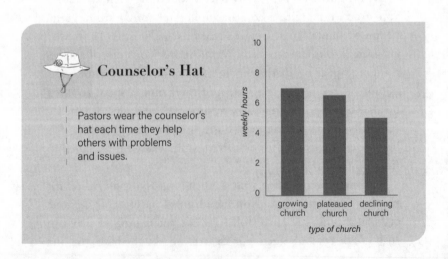

Counselor's Hat

Pastors wear the counselor's hat each time they help others with problems and issues.

The Case of the Pastor-Chaplain. "I don't want the church to grow anymore," confessed Mike Milford. Pastor Mike's words bewildered Gladys George, his secretary. Mike was the founding pastor of Evergreen Baptist Church, which had grown in its first three years to 185 regular worshipers on Sunday morning. Most people in the church were thrilled about the recent growth, but, surprisingly, Pastor Mike was not one of them.

Gladys sat across the desk from Pastor Mike looking stunned. Quietly, she asked, "What do you mean?" "There's too many people," Pastor Mike retorted. "I have my hands full now trying to care for the people who are here. More people will mean more problems, and I can't handle it all."

Part of Pastor Mike's frustration was that his vision of shepherding people focused solely on caring for those who required or demanded it. In unguarded moments, he often told others, "The squeaky wheel gets the grease." When speaking in a more spiritual tone, he said, "I care for those to whom the Spirit directs me." If he had viewed *time* as a cherished resource, he might have taken a more proactive approach to shepherding.

Proactive or Reactive?

One of the most difficult challenges in wearing the counselor's hat is determining what to do with one's time during the day. No one typically holds pastors accountable for the use of their time. Thus, it's easy for pastors to wallow along ineffectively day after day, just waiting for the fire bell to ring so they can react—jump into action. No one sees that they are essentially doing nothing in particular most of the time.

Some pastors are proactive when it comes to sermon preparation. They have a set time to study, lay out a preaching calendar, and select topics well in advance. The notion of taking a proactive stance with caregiving, however, never enters their thinking. They are shepherds (firefighters) waiting for the sheep to call in a time of need (the bell to ring). Wearing the counselor's hat effectively means pastors must take seriously the most precious of all resources—time. Pastors must say, "Given my limited resources, the most precious of them being my time, with *whom* or on *what* should I be spending it?"[1]

Types of People

A helpful way of analyzing with whom you should spend time starts with acknowledging that people in your church are either VIPs, VTPs, VNPs, or VDPs.

Everyone knows that VIPs are *very important people*. They are the ones in your church who lead others to accomplish the vision and goals of ministry. VIPs embody your church's core values and model the way for others to follow.

VTPs in your church are *very trainable people*. Many are engaged in some sort of service, with some in leadership positions. They are those who are FAT—faithful, available, and teachable.

VNPs are *very nice people*. Your church would be a poor place without them. They attend worship services on a regular schedule, give money to the offerings, and support the church's ministry programs. They speak about Christ to their family and friends and invite them to church when the opportunity arises.

VDPs are *very draining people*. Some are critics of your ministry, while others are highly needful folks who require extra care and grace. Many are those who need special care for a limited time, for example, those seeking premarital counseling or ones who just need a short conversation over coffee. What they all have in common is the way they drain energy from most pastors.

Looking at the life of Christ through the lens of these descriptions reveals a fascinating picture of where he spent his time. Admittedly, the Bible gives only a selected perspective on the life of Jesus, but using what we know, Jesus divided his time as follows:

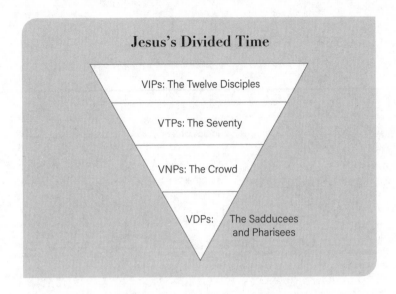

Jesus spent little time with the very draining people. He listened to the critics and responded to the needy but never let either of them control or divert his time away from larger goals. Plus, Jesus expended just a little more time with crowds of people. His feeding of the five thousand is one example. Giving time to larger crowds of people was necessary, as many of them were good people moving toward greater commitment to him and his message. It was the pool out of which trainable people were discovered and recruited. By far, Jesus dedicated most of his time to those who were open to his message and trainable for future leadership: the seventy and the twelve. He sent the seventy out on mission, and he lived his life with the twelve. Fundamentally, Jesus gave most of his time to those who ministered to others (VIPs and VTPs) and less to those who needed ministry (VNPs and VDPs).

If you apply this perspective to your own ministry, where are you investing your time? To whom should you be giving your time? For most pastors, the best division of time should look something like the following:

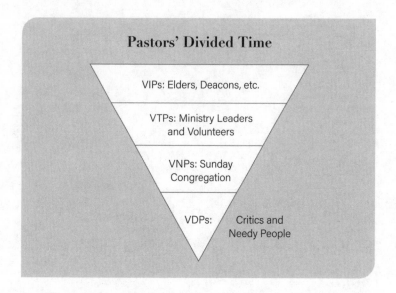

The main point is that you must think intentionally about the use of your time. Wearing the counselor's hat properly requires taking intelligent initiative in setting boundaries on your time.

DR. MC SEZ

If you visit your local bank or credit union, you may run into the president in the lobby. She will shake your hand, welcome you, and say how happy she is to have you as a client. You'll be appropriately impressed and go away thinking it's a great bank. If the president doesn't take your money, it won't bother you; that's the teller's job. If she doesn't help you fill out a loan application, it won't matter; that's the loan officer's job. Indeed, if you don't see the president again for a couple of years, you won't care. You have been favorably disposed to the bank because of that short meeting with the president.

Similarly, average church attendees today don't expect as much from a pastor as they did in the past. As a pastor, however, you should cultivate a strategic presence when wearing the counselor's hat. Here are some ideas on how to do so.

1. **Walk slowly through the lobby.** Some pastors hide out before, between, and after worship services. Being in the green room may be comfortable, but you'll have a more strategic presence if you walk through the lobby, taking time to greet and speak with people. You don't need to engage in long conversations; just take time to speak with a few. Not everyone will get to talk with you, but everyone will know that you are there.

2. **Listen and ask questions.** Focus on the person you're talking to, and resist looking past them to the next person. Learn to say, "I'm sorry," "I don't know," "I'm happy for you," "How can the church help?" "Will you forgive me?" and "I forgive you."

3. **Thank people for their concern, but don't promise results.** When people share a criticism, nicely explain that you can't do anything about the issue. Encourage them to talk to the right person or department. If they share a need, point them to the right ministry, or have them call the office and make an appointment to talk to you later. Resist the urge to jump right to an answer or provide a solution in the moment.

4. **Thank people for their service to Jesus and your church.** A few words of appreciation will empower most people for a long time. Small, handwritten notes carry powerful aromas of care in today's digital world.

5. **Make strategic appearances.** Be present with people at key moments. Remember: funerals are mandatory; weddings are optional. Know your people and culture, and show up at key times.

6. **Make pastoral phone calls.** Make one phone call a day to a randomly selected person who attends your church. Keep the conversation short, ask how they are doing, let them know you care about them, and thank them for being part of the church. Talk to whomever answers the phone. If it's a little child, teenager, or other family member, talk with them.

7. **Get out of the office.** Book at least one or two appointments a week with people to talk about real-world issues. Meet near places where people work. Don't talk about the church or church issues but discuss life in the real world. Focus on what is pressing in on their lives. Ask what they cry about, what they rejoice about, their work, families, and friends.

What Are You Doing?

Determining whom to spend time with is a beginning, but you must also think about what you should be doing.

The Case of the Expectant Deacon. "When are you going to mow the lawn, Pastor?" The question astonished Pastor Miller. He had served Crossroads Church for only three weeks. The lawn around the church was fairly long, but he never imagined he was responsible to mow it. In his previous church, that had been the job of the trustees. His conversation with Deacon Fenton was a jolt.

"Is that what you hired me to do?" Pastor Miller's response sent a reverse shock wave back to Deacon Fenton. "Well . . . ahh . . . I've never thought about it," Deacon Fenton acknowledged. "The previous pastors always mowed the lawn, and I just assumed you'd do it too."

I doubt if most people in a congregation, or church leaders for that matter, have even considered Pastor Miller's question: "Is that what you hired me to do?" Pastors and church leaders need to step back and ask, "What is the pastor's primary responsibility?" Beyond the responsibility to pray (1 Tim. 2:1–8) and preach the Word (2 Tim. 4:2), what are pastors to do?

Being a shepherd is closely aligned with being a friend. It's within friendships that the best advice, rebuke, comfort, and correction are made and accepted. A therapist may be in a person's life temporarily, but a pastor is in their life for the long haul. Pastors customarily build on strong, existing relationships. When you've buried a person's mother, baptized their children, and officiated at their nephew's wedding, you have been in their life consistently. That gives you an open door for caregiving that few others enjoy.

Most pastors are not psychologists. Unless you're a trained therapist, you probably don't know much about ADHD, PTSD, OCD, schizophrenia, or repressed memories. You must remember, though, that the prefix *psych* means *soul*. Psychology is the study of the soul, and who can do that better than pastors?

When wearing the counselor's hat, pastors find they are most often asked to work through five crucial issues: grief, divorce, suicide, addictions, and marriage problems. To do so, pastors and churches use one or more of the following approaches.

Pulpit care. Pastoral care is provided through the Sunday sermons, pastoral prayer, and after service prayer. Some pastors have a unique ability to love people from the pulpit, while providing helpful counsel for life's struggles and challenges. It's certain that the Bible covers a plethora of issues, which can be helpful. The opportunity to visit privately with a prayer counselor following a worship service offers a personal touch that meets many needs.

Lay ministry care. Volunteers who have special interests and gifting in caring for others can be organized into small teams who visit, pray for, and care for others. Expanding a church's care ministry through multiple teams widens effective caregiving beyond what a single pastor can do on their own.

Assistant pastor care. A staff position may also be created to center on caring for others in the congregation. In some cases, a retired pastor is hired to fill this position part-time. In larger congregations, a specialist in counseling or general pastoral care is brought onto the staff to target people's needs.

Small group care. Larger churches discover that expecting all pastoral care to come from staff pastors is unworkable. The answer is to encourage the expansive growth of a small group ministry with caregiving at its heart. No matter what the groups are called—home groups, care groups, grace groups, mini-churches, care cells—their main job is to provide TLC: tender loving care.

Referral care. Staff pastors or designated laypeople offer triage meetings in order to determine the nature of needs. They then provide resources and means to direct people to professional and community organizations for help.

Which of these five practices do you use? Which ones are the most helpful? Which ones will you develop in the years to come?

The Case of the Bishop of the City. Pastor Steve started Rancho Community Church in a smaller town of five hundred residents, with just eight families. Over the next thirty-eight years, the city grew just past one hundred thousand residents, and the church grew to serve two thousand people. During those years, Pastor Steve discipled, baptized, buried, trained, counseled, and visited so many people that he became the de facto bishop of the city. Yet, as the church grew, he instinctively realized he couldn't continue to counsel and care for everyone. Taking Ephesians 4:11–12 seriously, Pastor Steve equipped others to do the bulk of the pastoral caregiving. He was always available to care for major emergencies, but others shared the load, which allowed him to wear other hats besides the counselor's.

Like Pastor Steve, be sure to keep in mind that all believers (not just you!) are responsible for providing care. Speaking about his return and the judgment between the sheep and the goats, Jesus says, "For I was hungry, and you gave Me something to eat; I was thirsty, and you gave Me something to drink; I was a stranger and you invited Me in; naked, and you clothed Me; I was in prison, and you came to Me" (Matt. 25:35–36). He is speaking these words to all the righteous sheep, not just the pastors. It's everyone's duty to care for others. The apostle James tells all true Christians, "Pure and undefiled religion in the sight of our God and Father is this: to visit orphans and widows in their distress" (James 1:27). The honest work of faith is to provide what is necessary to brothers' and sisters' well-being (2:15). Consequently, be sure to build teams of people to help you provide pastoral care.

The nerve center for pastoral care is equipping the saints for ministry (Eph. 4:12). This starts with transforming cared-for Christians into caring Christians. Those who are gripped by caring love—who have experienced love and care from others—are often the prime people to enlist in care ministry. Yet, simply being a Christian does not make one a caring person, nor will just knowing the Bible make one a caring person. It takes some level of training. Training is needed in at least four pivotal areas so that care ministry leaders can provide:

- **COMFORT** for the hurting—one-to-one support and grief ministry
- **ASSISTANCE** for the needy—benevolence and crisis relief
- **RECOVERY** for the addicted—addiction ministry and care groups
- **ENCOURAGEMENT** for the aged—convalescent and homebound ministry

In order to effectively train others, you have to see the good of the total church as more important than yourself. You have to resist the tendency to protect your job and position by personally caring for everyone. To use a military analogy, you must change from a frontline medic for wounded Christians to a behind-the-line trainer of medics. As long as you hold on to the practice of being the primary caregiver, there will be negative consequences.

1. The quality and quantity of care will be limited by your own limited capacity.
2. The church will be limited in its ability to grow by providing qualitative and quantitative care for the souls of people.
3. It will create an unhealthy dependency and codependency between pastor and people
4. You will damage yourself physically, spiritually, emotionally, and relationally.
5. You won't have time to carry out your role of equipping the saints for ministry.

So, if you want to wear the counselor's hat well, quit being a chaplain and get into the battlefield of ministry by equipping the saints to do the work of caregiving. How? The best way to begin is to lead your own care group. One-on-one training and classes may be effective, but Jesus is never seen working with people one-on-one. Rather, he is always in a group. Small group caring may be the best way to arouse the interest and concern of others. Why not start a care group this month?

Telling Time or Building Clocks?

A time teller is a pastor who wears the counselor's hat extremely well. Because this pastor provides excellent pastoral care, the church relies on the pastor to be at the bedside of every sick person, at each counseling session, and available at any time of need. Clock-building pastors wear the counselor's hat by equipping others to tell time. The care ministry of the church goes on even in their absence, since they are not the only ones who can tell time, that is, give care. When you wear the counselor's hat, are you telling time or building a clock?

DR. MC SEZ

As you put on the counselor's hat, here are some essential principles I've found helpful.

1. **Use the Bible in your caregiving.** There is no better resource or tool than Scripture. It's "living and active and sharper than any two-edged sword, and piercing as far as the division of soul and spirit" (Heb. 4:12). It judges the thoughts and intentions of the heart.
2. **Jesus is the Savior; you aren't.** Don't swallow the savior hook, when you try to take the place of Jesus in another person's life. When people start free-falling into grief or despair, you can be a caring companion but not their parachute. Another way to put it: God cures; we care.
3. **Pastors are general practitioners.** Defer people to specialists. In most situations, don't meet more than two or three times with

people. If you can't solve their problems in those few meetings, you're better off referring them to someone better trained.

4. **You are not a garbage can.** Be careful when people use you for negative carping, complaining, grousing, and gossiping. If people come with sincere needs, take the time to minister to them. Don't allow them to dump on you for no reason other than for their own enjoyment.

5. **Pay the rent.** Do whatever caregiving is necessary to establish trust. It's necessary and needful to care for souls. Even if the counselor's hat is not your favorite one, you must wear it occasionally as part of your responsibility. Always treat needy and hurting people with dignity. They are created in God's image and deserve respect.

6. **Remember that seldom is the urgent important or the important urgent.** Don't feel like you have to play a game of pastor-fetch, like some dog playing with a ball. Some members of your congregation will expect you to jump and chase their agenda at every request or command. Don't fall into that trap. Have the courage to say no to some things, so you can say yes to better things.

7. **Just be there.** In difficult times, you may not know what to say, but just be there. Pastors often have a lot of just-be-there days. Particularly in smaller churches, this means helping with fences, painting barns, moving furniture, drinking tea or coffee, eating ice cream or pie, etc. At times, you may feel like your time is wasted in doing little of importance. If you want people to listen when you preach, however, just be there. The essential skill used when wearing the counselor's hat is to give and receive love. When nothing more can be done, being there is enough.

Where's the Pastor?

A question that's regularly heard in churches where pastors are enlarging the ministry of care is, "Where's the pastor?" This question arises when assistant staff or laypersons visit someone in the hospital, convalescent center, or home. It seems that most people want *the* pastor to show up and are disgruntled when they don't appear.

The real issue is visibility and accessibility. People want to believe they can talk to the pastor if they need to. If they see the pastor talking to others (see "walk slowly through the lobby" above), they realize they can speak to their pastor if they desire, because the pastor is visible.

Historically in the United States, people compared their pastor to the country doctor. In those bygone days, country doctors made house calls, charged little to nothing for their services, and were available at all times of the day and night. Nowadays, people more often compare their pastor to the compassionate leader of their company or business. They know it may be difficult to get an appointment with them, but they also realize they can see them if they wish, even though it may take time to get on the calendar.

A pastor's personality plays into perceptions of visibility and accessibility too. Some pastors have warm and caring personalities, while others come across as cold and uncaring. Soft skills, or a lack thereof, can make or break a pastor in any church. It's commonly known that churches hire for hard skills (preaching, teaching, administration) but fire for lack of soft skills (empathy, etiquette, warmth). Look at the biblical requirement for elders in 1 Timothy 3:1–7. Do most of the requirements involve hard skills or soft skills? Most are soft skills such as being gentle, hospitable, and respectable. Good soft skills are essential when you put on the counselor's hat. A warm smile, a listening ear, eye contact, a friendly demeanor, and pleasant body language are all elements that communicate you are accessible. These skills can be learned, developed, and improved over time. They make you accessible.

While some church attendees may desire your physical presence—and only *your* presence—most probably won't. What they'll want, however, is seeing you visibly present *and* accessible if needed in an emergency. It's therefore wise to have the counselor's hat nearby so you can put it on in an emergency. But in general, developing some of the five methods for providing care noted previously is all that is needed.

I recall reading a penetrating story about pastoral care a few years ago. A pastor was complaining to a woman in his church about the burden he was carrying of pastoral care. After listening patiently to his whining, she interrupted. "I'm a nurse, and sometimes I have to carry bed pans. When I do, I carry them like a queen." Having to carry the bed pans of pastoral care will never cease in churches for pastors. So, when you wear the counselor's hat, wear it royally!

For Further Reading

Classic: Larry Crabb and Dan Allender. *Encouragement: The Key to Caring*. Grand Rapids: Zondervan, 1990.

Newer: Jason Cusick. *Five Things Any Congregation Can Do to Care for Others*. Indianapolis: Wesleyan Publishing House, 2009.

7

The Student's Hat

What is the major challenge of every leader? It is leading yourself! Pastors can't lead until they've led themselves. In the concrete world, this means the truly faithful pastor never graduates but is a perpetual student. By wearing the student's hat, pastors illustrate that leaders are learners. They know they must continually upgrade their knowledge, skills, and abilities on a regular basis. The graduation hat is a bit misleading. Fruitful pastors know they, or their associates, never graduate. Rather, they remain undergraduates of the great campus of local church ministry. What got them to where they are today will not get them to where they want to be tomorrow. It's true! Growing churches are led by growing pastors.

The Case of the Passive Pastor. Pastor Lester Bolles shivered as he woke. Startled to find himself sitting in his desk chair, he haltingly realized he'd been daydreaming. Affairs at church were okay. Nothing spectacular was happening, which was commonplace. The good news? Nothing bad was occurring either. By most barometers of ministry, Pastor Bolles was pleased with the church he served.

Still, he engaged in fantasy daydreaming about what his church might look like if it gambled more. Internally, he didn't like the word *gamble*. Perhaps *adventure* was a better word to use. Yes, that was it. He wondered what the church would be like if it approached ministry as an adventure. What if the church ran the risk of innovating fresh approaches to ministry? How exciting it could be to lead a church that plunged headlong into adventuresome ministry.

To lead such a church, he'd need to take risks too. But why? Overall, activities at church were going well, with no conflict, few disgruntled people, and smoothly functioning programs. Why stir up trouble? While Pastor Bolles enjoyed the thrill of leading a church that engaged in huge leaps of faith, the thrill was always in his daydreams, never in reality. "Oh well," he sighed, leaning back in his comfortable desk chair, "everything will work out for the best."

Pastors who put on the student's hat are never passive. They don't sit at their desks week after week and assume everything will work out for the best. They don't sit and gaze at the scenery out their office windows. They don't live with the situation—good or

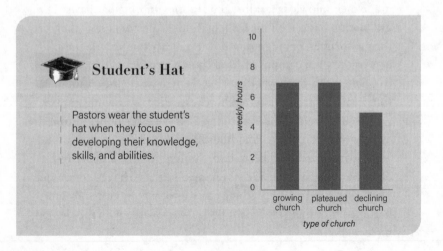

Student's Hat

Pastors wear the student's hat when they focus on developing their knowledge, skills, and abilities.

bad—but shake things up by growing themselves. Pastors in both growing and plateaued churches wear the student's hat two hours more per week than those in declining churches.

Leading Yourself

You must lead others, yes, but lead yourself first. Here are five reasons pastors must lead themselves.

First, people holding the position of pastor in today's or tomorrow's church will find it necessary to upgrade their knowledge and skills on a regular and continuing basis. Once upon a time (like many mythological stories begin), a three- or four-year seminary education prepared a pastor for a forty-year ministry career. The root of the word *seminary* is the Latin *seminarium*, which means "seed bed." The idea is that a seminary education provides the seed that will grow into a lifelong ministry. This was true for many years when life changed at a slower pace. In the rapid-paced, changing world that pastors today function in, seminary by itself is not enough. Changes take place at breakneck speed. Each week, innovative technology emerges to challenge the way we relate, communicate, organize, and plan. The passive learner quickly falls behind. At best, today's seminary or Bible school education prepares pastors for ten years of ministry. Remember: you must reeducate yourself every decade to stay current with life and ministry.

Second, you have to take responsibility for your own growth and development. It'd be helpful if your church took responsibility to help you learn and grow. Regrettably, this rarely happens. While businesses spend billions of dollars a year to train and retrain their people, only the best-of-the-best churches invest any money in the training of their pastors. If you don't take responsibility for your own growth and development, likely no one will. So ask yourself questions: "Do I know what I'm doing?" "Do I have a sense of where I'm going?" "Do I feel out of touch with ministry today?"

Stop being passive about your own personal growth. Remember: you can't shrink your way to leadership.

Third, the broader the range of your responsibilities, the more significant your continued training becomes. Although it's critical that continuing education be encouraged for children's pastors or youth pastors, it's doubly important that senior pastoral leaders keep learning too. Lead pastors (senior or solo) regularly are bogged down wearing so many hats that they neglect their own development. Progress begins when you take time to invest in yourself. Remember: you have to train up to stay up.

Fourth, you must have a deliberate self-improvement plan. Such a plan must include getting away from your church and ministry—the daily, weekly, and monthly routine—so you can stand back and view them from a wider and deeper perspective. You must plan and calendar your personal growth as thoughtfully as you do your normal work schedule. Such a plan isn't easy, and it takes self-discipline. Open your calendar right now. Are there scheduled appointments for your personal development? Do you see any scheduled interviews with other leaders or time for reading? Remember: what gets on your calendar gets done.

Fifth, you can't manufacture the desire to learn. The motivation for continual self-improvement must originate from inside yourself. No hodgepodge of learning techniques, books, blogs, or classes will take the place of your personal desire to learn, grow, and advance in your field of ministry. Pastors who can't motivate themselves can't be motivated by any outside forces. Remember: leaders are learners!

Best Practices

Pastors wear the student's hat well by employing some of the following best practices. It begins with an internal look to discover your true self. To begin, wrestle a bit with the following questions.

- How much do I understand about what's happening in my church and the world in which we exist?
- How prepared am I to deal with the complex issues that confront my church and ministry?
- Where is my church headed in the next decade?
- What do I need to learn in order to lead my church for the next ten years?
- Where do I need to grow and develop in order to lead my church for another decade?

Answering these questions (and more to come, honestly) will get you started on wearing the student's hat. Consider the following suggestions too.

Determine Your Life Purpose

Close your eyes and imagine you're at your funeral. Now, this is not a morbid exercise. Just allow yourself to think about what you hope people will say about you at your funeral. Then in twenty-five words or less, summarize what you hope you'd hear into an overall life purpose or mission statement. As an example, this is my personal life purpose: My purpose in life is to love God, love my wife, and love my children. Obviously, this is just a summary with a lot of emotions, hopes, and dreams packed into it. I can expand on this easily. To love God means to develop a close relationship with Jesus Christ, to be the best I can be in my fields of work and service, to honor God in all that I do, and much more. Every phrase of my life purpose declares the need for self-improvement. I'll always need to improve in my love for God, my love for my wife, and my love for my children (which now includes grandchildren, daughters-in-law, and other extended family).

Write down your life purpose in a notebook or on your computer. Read it out loud. It sounds like something to grow into, right? Where do you need to grow? In what ways do you need to develop? How must you improve in your skills and relationships to fulfill your life purpose?

List the Ten Most Important Things

Make a list of the ten things in life that are most important to you right now. It may help to divide up the important things into categories like spiritual/devotional, spouse/family, health/exercise, wealth/retirement, career/ministry, plus a general one. Then, next to each item, write down two or three ways that you can advance or enhance each one. These become self-improvement goals. As you work on them, you are leading yourself.

Get to Know Yourself

Hold up a mirror and look at yourself. What are your unique strengths? Your unique weaknesses? What makes you angry, sad, or worried? How do you define success? Sometimes there is no better mirror than an old friend who will tell you the truth in a loving manner.

Once you've determined the answers to these questions, you'll be tempted to work on improving your weaknesses. While that is not a bad decision, it's not the wisest one. We are unlikely to make our weaknesses a strength. Wise and successful leaders point out that it's best to work on growing your strengths, while staffing people around you to care for your weaknesses. What are your top two or three strengths? How can you begin to design a growth program to enhance those strengths?

Build Yourself Broadly

Fruitful pastors of the future must be well-rounded people. You might put it this way: knowledge enriches knowledge, and the greater the variety of knowledge, the greater the enrichment. Pastors may be specialists in wearing the counselor's hat and will work hard to improve their understanding of pastoral care. However, if that's all they read or study, they'll limit their ability to lead. While they may be a specialist in pastoral care, it'll still be good to have some expansive knowledge of financial management, preaching, exposition, and other disciplines. Lead pastors may be specialists, but it's better if they are specialists-plus—that is, specialists with a wider body of knowledge.

Such a broadening process happens by design. You'll want to focus on your strengths, but don't neglect the larger growth of your entire person. Ask yourself: Do I have time for random soul searching? Do I have time for self-renewal that is not directly related to my ministry? Do I have time for outside activities (art, sports, reading, music, etc.) that will enlarge my personhood? In the end, do you have a plan to strengthen your cultural enrichment and renewal that broadens your entire personhood as well as your skills?

Manage Your Time and Energy

How well do you manage your use of time? How well do you manage your energy (health, fitness, and rest)? How well do you manage your relational time (family, friends, vacations, days off, etc.)? Here's the truth: time management is just self-management. No one can honestly manage time. Everyone has the same amount—168 hours a week! Here's a tip: use the *ABC technique*. Look over your week. If you have many things to do, divide them into three categories:

A—Must do
B—Should do
C—Can do

Put the As on your calendar and do them first. On the following week, start over with a new list, and divide it into the A, B, and C categories. Again, put the As on your calendar and do them first.

Keep doing this week after week. Your personal development is an A category, so be sure to make space for it on your calendar.

Leverage Mentorship

Find a mentor you can meet with at least monthly. Look for someone who is older than you as well as someone who has more experience than you. Ask to meet with them for breakfast or lunch (you pick up the tab), and make the time count by coming prepared with questions. A few mentors will meet with you a few times but may charge a fee for ongoing coaching. Some mentors will be in your life for a few months, others for a few years, and a tiny number for your entire life. Thank God for the time you have with each of them. One tip: ask a question and then listen. Remember, you're not meeting with a mentor to argue, press your point, or try to change their point of view. You're meeting to learn, and it's best to listen.

Practice downward mentoring too. Educational researchers have found an amazing fact. You learn about 10 percent of what you hear but about 90 percent of what you teach.[1] One way to develop your personal growth is to teach others. Find a way to teach others what you are learning. You'll find yourself growing quickly as a result.

DR. MC SEZ

Commit to continuous learning. Here are some tips that have helped me over the years.

- **Read, read, read.** Some of my friends (who are major leaders) read a book a week. For me, I've found that reading one hour in the evening is enough time to digest about one book a month. My focus is on biographies and books related to leadership, but I read widely. For example, I'm currently reading a book on the vice presidents of the United States. I just finished a book on the life of a famous musician and before that a book on advice from leaders. What are your reading habits? Do you read books, articles, blogs? Read twenty-five pages a day (about an hour a day). Put it on your calendar, and keep your appointment just like you would any other appointment.

- **Attend training events.** My habit for nearly four decades has been to attend at least one training event a year. The problem is there are so many conferences and seminars, how do you know which ones are the most beneficial? Here's a tip: before deciding on a conference or seminar, ask three people who have already attended how they rate it, or ask someone who has presented at multiple conferences to rate them. Did they learn anything new or helpful? Was the event all theory, or were there insights they could use immediately? What are your conference or seminar habits?

- **Listen to audio books or podcasts.** Since I commute a great deal by car, I've developed the habit of listening to audio books. So far, I've listened to books on the lives of George Washington, Abraham Lincoln, Benjamin Franklin, Malcolm X, Mark Twain, Albert Einstein, and Robert Kennedy, to name a few. As you can tell, my penchant is for biography. Yours may be some other interest. What are your listening habits? A tip: podcasts are popular today, but few are worth your time. Choose wisely!

- **Continue your formal education.** The popularity of doctor of ministry programs in seminaries is driven by the desire of pastors for continuing education. Pastors who have been out of school for ten years or more realize times have changed and so has ministry. Many return to school to catch up on what's been taking place in society, theology, and practical fields of ministry. What are your educational desires?

Red-Zone Learning

Leadership studies have found that leaders exist in one of three zones: green, red, and ultraviolet. The *green zone* is where you spend most of your time. Filled with predictable routines, it is warm, comfortable, and safe. The *red zone* is a sector of high risk. You find yourself challenged, stretched, and highly attentive to everything when in this zone. The *ultraviolet zone* is a realm of high duress. It's a place where you hunker down in a posture of self-protection. The hope is to live through it, not learn from it.[2]

The important aspect of the study for your personal leadership development is that learning goes up by 400 percent when you are in a red zone over being in a green zone. Functioning in the green zone is too easy. You may learn, of course, while you go about your day-to-day work, but it simply doesn't challenge you enough to create significant development. The other end of the spectrum creates too much duress. Working in the ultraviolet zone generates too much stress. Learning tends to shut down as you hold on to the end.

Do you genuinely desire to grow? The best way is to strategically put yourself in red-zone environments. How does that happen? It occurs when you find yourself in a place that demands more from you than normal. Think back to when you first started pastoring a church. You may have had one or two good sermons. However, once you started preaching weekly, you were stretched to prepare a new sermon weekly. The demand to formulate a new sermon every week stimulated a season of growth in your life. It tested your ability to exegete the Scriptures, find new illustrations, and apply principles to real life. You were in a red zone. The result? You grew by leaps and bounds. Over time, you designed a process and fell into a quite comfortable routine of preparing sermons, and you slipped into a green zone. You're no longer challenged to the same extent by preparing sermons. If all, or most, of your pastoral life is functioning in a green zone, you are not honestly learning and growing like you hope. The key is to strategically place yourself in red-zone situations. How can you do this? Here are a few ideas to get you started thinking.

1. **If you haven't gone on a short-term mission trip, do so.**
   Leading a team of people from your church to the mission field for a few weeks will stretch you immensely.

2. **Consider enrolling in a continuing-education program.** Go back to school to obtain a master's or doctoral degree. Doing so will impose new expectations on you. You'll be required to read broadly, which will arouse fresh thinking. Writing papers will cause you to formulate your ideas explicitly.

3. **Think about changing roles.** If you've served in one particular pastoral role for over ten years, you're most likely a bit rusty, maybe even bored. As a preaching pastor, consider sharing a significant part of the preaching with other staff members or elders. Use the extra time to become involved in another aspect of ministry. Are you an associate or assistant pastor? Consider exchanging roles with another staff member for a few months or a year.

4. **Get out of your office.** Do you prepare your sermons in your office at church? Move out of your office and start preparing your sermons at a local coffee shop. Take a few books with you, purchase a large cup of coffee, and sit at a table each Thursday and Friday morning while preparing your sermon. Do this for three months.

5. **Join a service club, gym, or volunteer organization.** Engage in something entirely outside your regular work. Get involved, meet people who don't attend your church, and discover their dreams and heartaches. Listen to outsiders. Learn their language.

These are a few ideas. I know you can think of more. Ask yourself, "Where and how can I achieve results that will make a difference within the next year and a half?" The answer must balance several things. The results should be hard to achieve. They should require "stretching," to use the current buzzword. But they also should be within reach.[3]

Do you want to be a fruitful pastor? Doing so is determined not by what you already know but by how fast you learn. It's not so much about how many tools and skills you have but about the high degree of flexibility and adaptability you can demonstrate. Red-zone learning helps you achieve these ideals. Remember: discomfort and challenge can produce great life change.

DR. MC SEZ

I've watched pastoral leaders for nearly four decades now. Here are some things I've noticed about how they wear the student's hat.

They are curious about everything. In their basic being, they seek to learn how things work, how to make things better, and how to be more successful in their ministry. It's more than curiosity, though— more what might be called *applied curiosity*. They seek to learn not simply to *know* but rather to *do* and *be*. Hence, they wring lessons from all their experiences and put what they learn to practice. They put the pieces together, connect the dots, and apply what they learn in positive ways.

They love a challenge. Effective leaders don't procrastinate, and they are drawn to the fire; they don't run from it. Adventure, danger (at least a little), and risk inspire the best in them. While they don't necessarily like conflict or confrontation, they don't shy away from what needs to be done. Furthermore, whether they win or lose, they learn.

They do something to enhance their personal growth *every day*. They might read a chapter of a book, send an email, make a phone call, schedule lunch with a mentor, listen to a podcast, ask questions of a newcomer, or reflect on their goals.

They do their job well, but they work on themselves. Rather than being concerned about the next church or the next position, they focus on doing their current ministry well. This doesn't mean they don't have dreams or godly ambition, far from it. Deeply held hopes and dreams pull them along. Nonetheless, they aren't serving to climb some sort of ladder of success, either. They do learn everything possible from their work, all while working on themselves.

They help people under them grow. They think not only about their own personal development but also about how to develop their team. They walk their talk by practicing what they preach—personal growth. This then gives them credibility to electrify others to spark their own strategic application of personal development.

They play in traffic. What I mean is, they push themselves out, participate, and get involved. They may not know the theory, but they gravitate to red zones naturally. You might say discomfort is their comfort zone. They believe that success is showing up, getting to work, and playing in traffic.

They agree with the statement "When you're through changing—you're through." Thus, learning to accept, create, and manage change is one of their top priorities. In a sense, they don't play to lose, but they play to win. They strive to grow mentally (read a book or take a class), physically (go to a gym or ride a bicycle), spiritually (meditate or pray), financially (save and invest), and culturally (visit museums or attend artistic performances). In other words, they seek to grow by enlarging their own world.

Lose or Learn

Every leader stumbles. When you do, you can either lose or learn. You can learn from your own mistakes or from the mistakes of others. Of course, the best way to learn is from the mistakes of others. That's why reading biographies of well-known leaders is so helpful. They all made mistakes—mistakes from which we can learn.

Former president John F. Kennedy is one of the most highly respected presidents of the United States. Paradoxically, he reached his highest level of popularity after he made a major mistake—the Bay of Pigs. It was what psychologists call a *strategic pratfall*. In laymen's terms, it means he fell on his butt! For those who don't remember, the Bay of Pigs was a failed invasion of Cuba by Cuban exiles who wanted to remove Fidel Castro from leadership. The US government covertly financed it, and its failure brought severe embarrassment to the Kennedy administration. It was a *strategic* pratfall because Kennedy took responsibility for it. His honesty demonstrated that he was not only human (he made a mistake), but he was also forthright in shouldering the responsibility.

Problems and difficulties never disappear from a leader's desk, but fruitful pastors learn to redeem them. A key part of learning, then, is to take responsibility for your own actions and not blame others. A successful apology includes an expression of regret, an explanation of what went wrong, an acknowledgment of responsibility, a declaration of repentance, an offer of repair, and a request for forgiveness. Giving a proper apology is a key skill all leaders must learn.

Slipping on a proverbial banana peel may make you feel like a failure, but it's a great opportunity to learn. It's akin to learning to ski or ice skate. If you're not falling down, you're not learning. For one thing, mistakes are often God's way of moving you in a different direction, or perhaps alerting you to areas in your life where you need to focus attention. For another thing, all leaders need a dose of humility every once in a while. At the heart of humility is the ability to learn from our mistakes.

One of the major discoveries from studies of leaders is how they learned from failure. In most situations, they never even use the word *failure*, preferring to use words like *mistake*, *glitch*, *bungle*, *false start*, *mess*, *setback*, and *error*.[4] No one can expect to go through a life of ministry without a major setback or failure. Indeed, where there is success and fruitfulness, there has to be failure. Redeem your failures, mistakes, or whatever you choose to call them, through an attitude of learning rather than losing.

God clearly works his will in spite of a leader's weaknesses (1 Cor. 1:18–31; 4:8–13; 2 Cor. 12:7–10). However, this fact doesn't remove your responsibility to grow and mature. In numerous places, Scripture admonishes us to grow. "Make your ear attentive to wisdom, incline your heart to understanding" (Prov. 2:2). Even Christ, we are told, "continued to grow and become strong, increasing in wisdom" (Luke 2:40).

Educators used to talk about kindergarten through high school (K–12). Then they spoke about K through college. With today's longer life spans and rapidly changing environments, it's better to talk about K–75, K–90, or K–100. You're never too old to learn. Adults can learn at all ages. Wearing the student's hat thus requires every pastor to think and behave like a perpetual student.

For Further Reading

Classic: John C. Maxwell. *Developing the Leader Within You*. Nashville: Thomas Nelson, 1993.

Newer: Aubrey Malphurs. *Maximizing Your Effectiveness*. Grand Rapids: Baker Books, 2006.

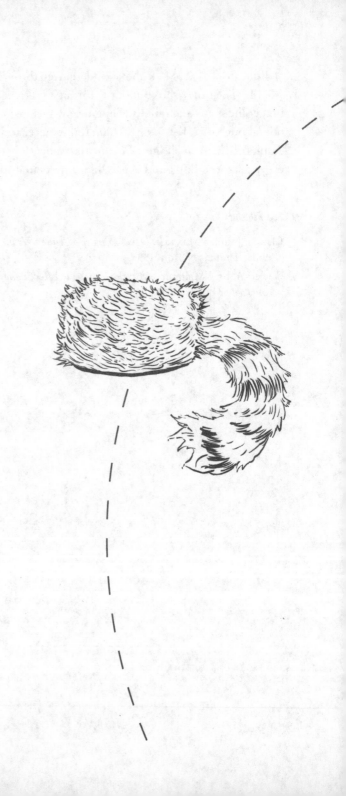

8

The Pioneer's Hat

The fur caps worn by America's early pioneers declared a desire and willingness to conquer the wilderness. Mountain men and women braved the unknown frontier of North America's wilderness to break new ground for farms, towns, and churches. Missionaries and evangelists, often called circuit riders, traveled on foot and horseback thousands of miles to spread the gospel message of salvation in Jesus Christ. They left families and gave up the prime years of their lives, but those who persevered bore eternal fruit.

When worn by the pastor, the pioneer's hat declares a desire and willingness to evangelize the lost by moving into new territory and doing ministry in new ways. No church, or organization of any type, can survive long unless it births new members. The entire human race would extinguish itself in about one hundred years if babies were not birthed daily. Likewise, without new Christians birthed through the gospel on a regular basis, churches face a slow decline. Pastors in growing churches wear the pioneer's hat three hours more per week (twice as much) than those in declining churches, and one and a half hours (33 percent) more than pastors in plateaued ones.

The Case of the Medicinal Church. "Pastor," Jim and Sally spoke with a concerned tone, "what we mean is you care more about people outside our church than those inside."

Pastor Powell tried to maintain a calm façade, but his emotions were whirling inside. "I don't understand," he stuttered as he talked. "When I started as your pastor two years ago, you gave me a mandate to reach the lost around the church. If my memory serves me right, Sally, you were a member of the pastoral search team that gave me that charge."

"That's correct," Sally noted with sadness, "but I didn't think you'd ignore those of us already in the church."

"Tell me more," Pastor Powell asked, just to give himself time to think.

"Well, Pastor," Jim explained, "our church is a place of healing to us. Sally and I both work in places where the people are unpleasant when it comes to spirituality. A few of our colleagues are downright hostile to the gospel. By Friday, we're both so hungry for Christian fellowship that church is our place of refuge. We need the church to be around our friends who believe the same way we do, to get some healing, and recharge before heading back to work on

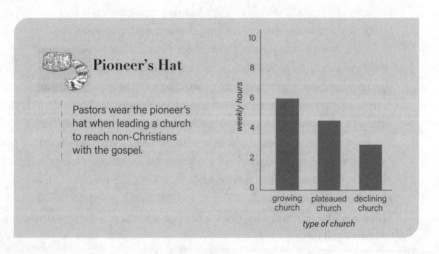

Pioneer's Hat

Pastors wear the pioneer's hat when leading a church to reach non-Christians with the gospel.

132

Monday morning. We appreciate your interest in evangelism, but lately it feels like you're more concerned about others than us. We just can't support your desire to reach the community any longer."

As North American culture glides toward secularism, significant numbers of church attendees view their church as a place where they gather in safety with others who hold similar beliefs and values. To them, the church is a home where they come each weekend to be healed, comforted, and encouraged before they venture back into an unfriendly world. Instead of being pioneers, venturing out to reach a lost world, numbers of churches have settled down to maintain the farm.

The nation of Israel is an example of a people who started out as pioneers and slowly became settlers. After years of moving from place to place in the desert, they were settled into a routine life. It was not always an enjoyable way of life but one the people had come to understand and accept. It was their way of life, and they were comfortable with it. Then, after forty years, God told Moses, "You have stayed long enough at this mountain. Turn and set your journey, and go to the hill country. . . . I have placed the land before you; go in and possess the land" (Deut. 1:6–8). After four decades of being settlers, it was time for the nation to become pioneers again.

In a comparable way, your church may be so comfortable that the people have lost their pioneering spirit. Face it! If you and your church have stopped pioneering, you're settlers. It's time to start pioneering again. Here's how to do it.

First, believe in the power of the gospel. Paul described how the Thessalonians received the gospel: "For our gospel did not come to you in word only, but also in power and in the Holy Spirit and with full conviction" (1 Thess. 1:5; see Rom. 1:16). The gospel of salvation through Jesus Christ is powerful because God is in it. When it's preached, God works through it to bring people to salvation. Yet, Paul makes it personal when he says "our gospel." He had made the gospel his own, and so must you if you hope to preach it with power. You must preach the gospel out of your own experience of saving grace. The power derives from your personal assurance that when you preach the gospel, the Holy Spirit is at work bringing salvation to those who hear and believe. The obvious question is, do you preach with full assurance that God will work through the preaching of the gospel to change lives?

Second, expect the gospel to bring growth when it is proclaimed. A metaphor the apostle Paul used throughout his epistles was of *seed that grows*. "I planted, Apollos watered," Paul declares, "but God was causing the growth" (1 Cor. 3:6). There is a living seed to sow—the gospel of salvation through the atoning death and resurrection of Jesus Christ (see 1 Cor. 15:1–11). When it's sown, God makes it grow. Luke reminds us, "The word of the Lord continued to grow and be multiplied" (Acts 12:24). Paul gave thanks for the Colossians because they believed when they "heard in the word of truth, the gospel" (Col. 1:5). He noted that the same gospel was "constantly bearing fruit and increasing" (1:6). Bearing fruit is an agricultural expectation. A sower always plants in anticipation of the seed growing. God makes the seed grow whenever it is planted in the hearts and minds of people. The obvious question is, do you sow the gospel in expectation of growth?

Third, encourage everyone in your church to demonstrate the gospel. The most powerful testimony to the gospel's power is changed lives, particularly where love is seen. The new commandment given by Jesus to his disciples was to "love one another." "By this," Jesus affirmed, "all men will know that you are My disciples, if you have love for one another" (John 13:34–35). Part of what gave the gospel power when preached to the Thessalonians was the loving relationships among all concerned. "We proved to be gentle among you, as a nursing mother tenderly cares for her own children," Paul noted. "Having so *fond an affection* for you, we were well-pleased to impart to you not only the gospel of God but also *our own lives*, because *you had become very dear to us*" (1 Thess. 2:7–8, emphasis added). The obvious question is, do your people demonstrate love for each other and lost people in the community?

Fourth, get your people out into the world to connect with unchurched people. Cultivate a sending mentality in your church. People outside your church have no interest in your world. You must connect with their world. Christ didn't say, "Hey! I'm up here in heaven. I hope you get interested in it." Rather, he came down to earth, entered our world, spoke our language, and felt our pain so that he could take us up into his world (see John 1:14; Heb. 2:17–18; 4:15). We need to do the same with people outside our church. They aren't interested in church. We must leave our hallowed halls and get into their world. The obvious question is, are your people entering the world of the unchurched?

Fifth, teach everyone in your church to be a contagious inviter. Andrew invited his brother Peter to meet Jesus, and Philip invited Nathanael. In both cases, the invitations resulted in them becoming disciples (John 1:40–51). On a personal level, non-Christians, as well as unchurched people, are open to discussing spiritual concerns. It's invitations to church that are not as well received as in the past. Your people must still invite others, but to dinner in their home, or lunch at a restaurant, or some social event. Ask your people to use these times to share how Christ has changed their own lives. Their relationships carry a greater impact than a sermon does. It's still a good idea to encourage your people to invite friends to worship services, but couple the invitations with bringing them. Bring friends to church, sit with them, take them to lunch, and discuss the spiritual principles you both hear that day. The obvious question is, do your people invite and bring the lost?

Sixth, focus your efforts on who you are trying to reach rather than those you are trying to keep. Narrow your focus from *everyone* to *someone*. You won't have a good outreach plan unless you can say specifically whom you're trying to reach. It's common to label such people a *target audience*. Now, before you criticize that terminology, remember they're not just targets but real people. Call non-Christians what you desire, but the more specifically you can describe them, the better your outreach efforts will be. The best *someones* you should focus on are the folks your church members are already doing life with—neighbors, friends, associates, and family members. Have your people take an inventory of those they do life with but are far from God. Those are your someones. The obvious question is, do you know who your someones are?

Seventh, make your church highly visible in the community. If non-believers have heard positive gossip about your church, it will help your attendees invite and invest in relationships. In our secular society, around 25 percent of people are not predisposed to think of church, let alone attend one.[1] What they are seeking is hope. Position your church as a place of hope, which means a place of healing, restoration, and redemption. Partner with community organizations to offer Easter egg hunts, tutoring classes, gasoline buy-downs, Fourth of July fireworks, games in the park, hot chocolate on cold Halloween nights, etc. The obvious question is, is your church well known for the hope it brings to the community?

DR. MC SEZ

In the early history of the United States, the Christian faith captured the minds and hearts of people, and this resulted in major movements of church planting, holiness, and missionary outreach. One of the difficult challenges of reaching people in a secular culture, however, is that we must re-evangelize rather than evangelize, which is more difficult. Here are some of the differences.

- In the initial years of evangelism, people believed in a moral law, knew they had transgressed it, and wanted to be forgiven. In our secular society, people no longer believe in a standard moral law, feel more shame than guilt, and don't think they need to be forgiven.
- In the initial years of evangelism, people were raised in an agrarian culture that accepted belief in a God who could be called upon in

136

times of disease, drought, or war. In our secular society, people no longer believe in a personal God who loves and cares for them.

- In the initial years of evangelism, people believed in a holy God who ruled the world justly. In our secular society, people, if they believe in God, project arrogant anger at him for allowing injustice to exist in the world.
- In the initial years of evangelism, people often had little exposure to Christianity. In our secular society, people have had just enough exposure to be inoculated against it.
- In the initial years of evangelism, people's understanding of Christianity was fresh, and they were more likely to have a clear understanding of the Christian narrative and beliefs. In our secular society, people have heard numerous versions of Christianity and are more likely to have mistaken views of Christianity that have to be unlearned.

So how do we go about re-evangelizing a secular people? The answer is conversation, conversation, and more conversation—particularly conversations that take place between friends. Thus, it's critically important to train your people to engage in evangelistic conversations with their near neighbors. Conversation is the only universal methodology for re-evangelizing people in a secular society that once was Christian.

Blaze the Trail

In the early nineteenth century, the First Industrial Revolution started North America on the trail away from an agrarian culture to an industrial society. The revolution was pushed forward by new inventions like water-powered mills and steam-powered trains. These new technologies changed the economic system, allowing for movement of resources and people in ways unheard of in the previous century. Between 1850 and 1900, as developing technology brought forth the Second Industrial Revolution, thousands of people moved from small, rural towns to large cities. What drew families to move were the new jobs available at plants and factories. The watchwords were industrialization and standardization. The birth of new communication systems (telegraph and telephone), power systems (water and electrical), and health systems (sewage and trash) allowed for the unprecedented growth of larger cities.

One of the challenges facing churches during those times was what to do with children in the summer months. In an agrarian society, children worked on the farm in the summer. The public-school calendar was built around the need for children to help during the planting and harvesting summer months. In the city, however, children wandered about aimlessly in the summer, since there were no crops to tend, cows to milk, or fences to mend. It wasn't long until innovative church leaders started offering daily Bible schools for children in the summer months. At first, these Bible schools were taught for several weeks and several hours a day. Over the years, they became well known as vacation Bible schools (VBS). Churches found in the larger cities of New York, Illinois, and Pennsylvania quickly adopted this new, innovative method for educating and evangelizing children, with the first formal VBS curriculum being published in 1923. The new ministry of VBS started with a person who stepped up in faith to innovate a new approach for reaching children. It was driven by the changing society around the church and propelled by a desire to find real solutions to real problems.

Pioneering innovation never stops. Jump ahead one hundred years and the S in VBS no longer means school. Today, S is for sports or science. Churches continue to teach the Bible to children in the summer, but now it's more likely to be integrated into a soccer camp, basketball camp, computer camp, science camp, music camp, drama camp, or a myriad of other camps. Themed camps are the innovation of the early twenty-first century.

When you put on the pioneer hat, you must engage ministry with an independent, pioneering spirit that willingly changes the S in VBS from school to sports or science. Of course, VBS is just one example, but as the pastor, you determine whether a church innovates or vegetates. Most pastors know this and have a stated policy that calls for the design of new programs and ministry. Unfortunately, there is a conflict between policy and practice. While it may be policy to invite innovation, it's church practice to resist it. What keeps numerous churches stagnant is that their approach to evangelism and outreach no longer works.

Throughout history, changes in society have driven changes in the church. Few local churches have a history that spans more than a hundred years, but the church has survived over two thousand years in part because it has adapted to changes around it. Whenever the status quo has been challenged, church leaders have become catalysts for change. Most people fail to see the necessity for change, but innovators perceive the challenge and feel the need to respond, as it was when VBS first developed years ago. A few people saw the need and responded with an innovative approach— Bible school in the summer.

That's why you need to wear the pioneer's hat. As you design ministry to fulfill God's mission for your church, you'll discover opportunities disguised as problems. Your best innovative ideas occur in response to those real problems. That's the definition of innovation: *designing new solutions to real problems for real people to reach God's mission for your church.*

So, how do you begin to blaze a trail of innovation in your church? Doing so requires us to think like pioneers. Here are some ideas to get you started.

Begin with diagnosis and analysis. Accept the truth that making disciples of secular people requires rethinking how ministry is accomplished. If your evangelism approach is obsolete, continuing to use it will not only be ineffective but also degenerative. As medical doctors will tell you, a degenerative disease will not be cured by procrastination. Analyze what's happening. Face facts. Decide to do something different.

Defy the tyranny of the past. You and your church have done many things right over the years. If this were not so, your church wouldn't be here. Nevertheless, it is here, which argues for the rightness and success of past ministries. Not only has your church done the right things, but they also were done well. Yet, while you continue to employ your best efforts, they're not bearing fruit today. It's time to try something new that will bless the past and improve the future.

Listen to diverse sources. Wearing the pioneer's hat requires the lead pastor to become a master listener. Seek out innovative leaders in the church world and outside of it. Find people who don't relate well in the present but are mentally living in the future. You want to listen to those who ask, "What if?" rather than, "What is?" Read what they write. Listen to what they say. Learn how they think. Define the principles behind the methods. Then, apply the principles to your own ministry.

Partner with young thinkers. Sometimes this will be younger people, but don't forget that older folks often think young. You'll learn quickly that there are some old young people and some young old people. It's how they think, not how long they've lived. There's no getting around the reality that younger people are always more on the cutting edge of change and innovation than older people. We all fall in love with the technology or methodologies that were new when we were younger. Our emotional investment in those old approaches can slow down our ability to adapt and flex. Find others who understand the future and are agile and flexible in how they think about ministry.

Affirm pioneers. Bless new ideas, as well as the people who come up with them. If you ignore people with innovative ideas, they'll quit coming to you. Worse, if you dismiss them and their ideas, they'll leave your church. Tell people on your ministry team that you expect them to try five new approaches this year. Then, bless their efforts when they do it. Take responsibility for things that don't work well and give credit to the innovator when things go well.

Do the right things first. The temptation in ministry is to ignore the old, routine ways of doing ministry in favor of the new, exciting ways. Innovation arises from hearts and minds that are already doing things well. Make sure you are fulfilling the routine aspects of ministry well before you succumb to the pull of the new. The routines are the stuff of life for the church. If you're doing old things well, the congregation will give you permission to try new things.

Start something new. An old principle of growth avows that it takes new units for new growth. The idea is that old ministry approaches are not sufficient for reaching new people, which is a reality most pastors and churches are coming to see. Now, don't just do something new for its uniqueness. Only try innovative ideas that advance your church's mission.

Experiment out of sight. Package your fresh ministry approaches as experiments. If they work, you're home free. If they don't work, oh well; it was just an experiment. Your people all know that scientific experiments often fail, but also that with enough experiments, eventually something good is discovered. Along with this, do your experiments out of view. New medicines are brought to the market every year, but few of us ever see inside the lab. Similarly, if possible, start innovative ministries where they are not in full view of the entire congregation. This allows you to protect your people from critics who may sink the new idea before it has a chance to work.

Keep trying. A culture of innovation doesn't develop overnight, nor do innovative ministries. It takes consistency, dedication, and persistence over time. In some cases, it may take four to five years before an innovation approach takes hold. The truth is that churches rarely change quickly through immediate innovations. Rather, they change slowly over time. Stay committed to discovering and trying new approaches to ministry. In time, some of them will succeed, while the mistakes will fade into oblivion.

Build on the spillover effect. When you establish one or two excellent, innovative ministries, other ministries and people will rise to the same level. Success breeds success.

Know church history. The longer you live and observe church history, you begin to realize that not much is new. Sure, the forms change (as they should), but the functions remain the same—prayer, worship, evangelism, fellowship, etc. Knowing recent church history, as well as the ancient, guides you to see the possibilities and the impossibilities. This will aid you in analyzing which innovations support your mission and which ones don't.

Ground it in Scripture. You know this, but it's worth saying again. Innovations must be grounded in Scripture. The purpose of innovation is not simply to change things so we're not so bored. Instead, innovation is a way to push forward the mission of God in making disciples. All revivals took place in part because some innovative person took the message of the Bible, put it into the language of the people, and delivered it in a form to which they could relate.

DR. MC SEZ

Being able to innovate is a necessary attribute of fruitful ministry in today's changing world. Some churches seem to thrive on change, while others fear it. Here are a baker's dozen factors to keep in mind as you work to develop a culture of innovation in your church.

1. **Look at innovation as an opportunity to improve yourself, your team, and your church.** Embrace the need for change, and help others see it as good too. Set your affections not just on present practices but also on future possibilities.
2. **Maintain a healthy curiosity in new methods.** As a leader, you must keep abreast of developments in your field of work. Keep a sharp eye out for reports, technologies, new ideas, and innovations that others are using. Then, adapt them to your own people, place, and problems.
3. **Speak positively about other pastors who are doing ministry differently than you.** You don't have to agree with everything done in other churches, but it's unwise to verbally reproach them. If people

around you criticize other churches or pastors for the new ways they are doing ministry, always answer, "Here, our church has its own problems to solve. If you don't like what (insert name) is doing, send them an email (or letter or phone call)."

4. **Learn to let go of your cherished ways of doing ministry.** You'll always be more comfortable with the old and familiar ways of ministry, particularly with the methods with which you were personally discipled. In today's climate, however, holding on too long can be deadly.

5. **Pinpoint a top five.** One key to successful innovation is to pinpoint areas where change is clearly needed. Accurately identifying your top five problem areas and innovating fresh ideas for addressing these areas will give you a chance of successful results. Poorly targeted innovations result in increased resistance to future change.

6. **Partner with those more innovative than yourself.** You may not be the most creative person on your team, nor for that matter the most effective evangelist. Find those who are better than you, and work with them to create fresh ways to reach the unchurched. Give them the credit for what works and take the blame for what doesn't.

7. **Stay flexible.** Stay away from putting in place rules, policies, and guidelines that smother creative innovation. Too-rigid adherence to church protocols causes ministries to be stymied and stalled. Reduce lines or levels for approval. Trust your team to make wise innovations in their own areas of ministry.

8. **Keep people informed about changes that may affect them.** A lot of resistance to innovation comes from people not understanding why, when, and how new ministry approaches will work.

9. **Exhibit confidence in your team.** Make it okay for them to make mistakes. If you show doubts about your team members, they'll lose the confidence that is needed to try new innovations. Mistakes are building blocks, the price you'll pay for improving your ministry.

10. **Broaden your perspectives.** Expose yourself and your team to new ideas outside of their day-to-day experience. Even the best people get into ruts of repetition and comfort. Break into your team's world by encouraging them to exchange ideas with leaders in other fields or read about and discuss new ways of ministry. Bring in

guests to expand their thinking. Do whatever you can to counter the tendency toward routinization of ministry.

11. **Cherish dissatisfaction.** There's a tendency among pastors to surround themselves with sunshine spreaders, i.e., chronic optimists. It's good to look in the shadows sometimes too. That's where you'll discover the most need for innovation. Complaints sometimes point the way to future innovation.

12. **Dredge up old ideas.** Innovative ideas die a premature death in many churches and are buried alive. A ton of untapped ideas likely lie buried in the minds of your team. Urge them to dig deeply into their dream banks for abandoned ideas they think are worth refreshing. You may find some diamonds buried there.

13. **Disappear.** Get away from the familiar. You will find that getting away from it all is an excellent way to stimulate fresh thoughts. When fresh insights aren't coming your way, a change of scenery often brings them to the surface. Ask God to reveal insights to help you fulfill his mission in your church, and then vary the places you go and the people with whom you associate. You may find insights in visiting other churches, or talking with people in a coffeehouse, or observing people in a hotel lobby. If you desire to wear the pioneer's hat well, you must stop spending all of your time with people of your church, administrating the programs and staff. Rather, spend a large part of your time with the unchurched. New ideas often arise in new places and from new people.

Expiration Dates

Expiration dates are attached to nearly every product in use. You can find them on items ranging from food to tires to medicine. Of course, people continue to use outdated products, sometimes for years after they should have been replaced.

Now, you may not be aware of it, but church ministries have expiration dates too. It's just that no date is printed anywhere to let you know it. Most church ministries expire within fifteen years of their establishment. The normal pattern finds the most fruit in the initial five years, followed by good results in the second five, and a leveling off of impact in the final five years. Like people using products, churches continue to employ ministries even as they become ineffective. The primary way to overcome the lowering impact of older ministries is for you to put on the pioneer's hat. It may not come naturally or be your preferable hat to wear, but you must stand ready to lead your church to develop new ways of ministry.

For Further Reading

Classic: Joel A. Barker. *Paradigms*. New York: HarperCollins, 1992.

Newer: Larry Osborne. *Innovation's Dirty Little Secret*. Grand Rapids: Zondervan, 2013.

9

The Conductor's Hat

One of the fun things about watching high school and college football games is the halftime band performance. Bands march in lockstep across the football field playing their school's fight song. The sound of the drums and horns energizes the fans, but it's the intricate formations that delight them. Sections of the bands separate to the beat of the music, forming complex patterns, interweaving within each other, and crisscrossing through lines of performers.

Sophisticated maneuvers and dance moves cause audiences to clap with joy, but they don't happen by chance. In front of the band is a conductor who has selected the band members, chosen the music, designed the various maneuvers, and led them in practice. Occasionally, a field conductor or drum major marches along with the band in a visible position, but at other times, it's difficult to see the conductor. Having someone wear the conductor's hat, though, is crucial to the successful completion of the band's production. Without a conductor, it's unlikely that any band's performance would happen, and it surely would not happen as well as it does.

As a pastor, you wear the conductor's hat working with people of numerous talents, abilities, and skills. Directing people so that they work together in unity brings out the best in your church. Orchestrating the body so that action flows out of harmony is necessary to achieve the church's disciple-making mission. As conductor, you promote an environment that inspires people to serve and motivates people to participate. The essence of the conductor's hat is the ability to recognize ability in people and get them working in harmony with others. This hat is worn the most by pastors of plateaued churches (1.5 hours more than those in growing churches and 3.5 hours more than those in declining ones).

The Case of the Puzzled Pastor. "I just don't get it," Pastor Randy Gallo commented in puzzlement while holding the cell phone closer to his ear. "During the announcements this morning, I laid out a challenge to our people to get involved in some way. I described how it was their duty to serve, and then I presented statistics that demonstrated a clear need for several of our ministries. I even talked about how good it would feel to accomplish something for Christ." There was silence for a mo-

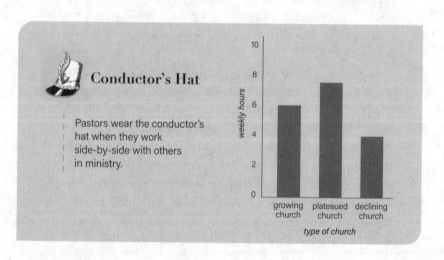

Conductor's Hat

Pastors wear the conductor's hat when they work side-by-side with others in ministry.

ment as he listened to what the other person was saying. Then he continued, "Yes, I gave a passionate plea to get involved in serving. I asked people to come and talk to me after the worship service if they'd like to volunteer." Pastor Gallo paused again to listen to his caller. "You guessed it. No one talked to me about serving. I felt like some people were even avoiding me. I've done everything I know of to motivate people to serve, but it's not working. I just don't get it."

Pastor Gallo's puzzlement is common among pastors and church leaders trying to wear the conductor's hat. Every effort to recruit and motivate new volunteers is met with silence, if not outright cold shoulders. People are so busy that they don't have time to serve, at least at church. They have time for work, friends, house projects, and, of course, their children's activities, but they have little time for church ministry. Fortunately, there are some keys for wearing the conductor's hat successfully.

Keys to Conducting

There are several keys to effective conducting.

First, know your mission. We are all aware that businesses have a financial bottom line. At first, we might think that churches don't have a bottom line, but that's incorrect. Churches do have a bottom line; it's just different. The bottom line of a church is changed people. While businesses seek to satisfy the customer, churches seek to change the person. When you think of it, that's what all nonprofit organizations seek—to change the person. A hospital seeks to change sick people into healthy ones. Schools seek to change students into educated adults. Churches seek to change people into followers of Christ—disciples who change their values into God's values and change their lives into godly ones.

Second, stay on mission. As a conductor, you have to learn to say no. There is always too much good to do and not enough resources to do it all. Any organization can only do a certain number of tasks. A major danger in smaller churches is to attempt more ministry than what resources can support. A major danger for larger churches is to take on things that don't fit their mission. Remember, God's kingdom encompasses both heaven and earth. Most nonprofit organizations focus all of their efforts on the earthly side of the kingdom. The church is the only organization that focuses on the other side of the kingdom—heaven. For that reason, many good causes and needs should not be your primary focus. The church has to keep touch with God's whole kingdom, but the church is not a food bank, or counseling center, or housing shelter, or any other strictly social service entity. Yes, you must keep touch with humanity and provide assistance where needed, but as a church, your focus is on changing lives, particularly bringing people into right relationship with Jesus Christ. If you allow yourself to get involved in too many good things, you'll lose focus.

Third, get others on mission with you. Pastors typically use five primary appeals to recruit and motivate volunteers: duty, logic, accomplishment, belonging, and caring. Last on the list today are duty and logic. Pastors using duty as a motivator usually talk about the importance of loyalty, commitment, and the obligation to use one's gifts. Using logic, pastors present statistics and analyze data, hoping it inspires others to serve where there is verifiable need. Next is motivational attempts based on challenges to accomplish something good for Christ and his church. Unfortunately, neither duty, logic, nor accomplishment of something valuable for Christ is a good motivator today. On the top of the list are caring and belonging. Recruiting people to care for others while becoming part of a caring group works the best.

Fourth, get others to play well. Conductors usually know how to play multiple instruments, but can you imagine a band conductor stepping off the rostrum and running back and forth among the band chairs, attempting to play every instrument? As crazy as that sounds, some pastors try to do so. The successful conductors are those who know their job is to build an effective team that will outlast them. They are the servants of the team. In place of trying to play every instrument, they recruit others who play better than they do.

Fifth, get others to play together. The role of a band conductor is to produce a fine-sounding piece of music. The problem is the various band sections see the specifics in different ways. The brass, the woodwinds, and the percussionists—all the instrumentalists—must perform well in order for the ensemble to produce a unified sound that is beautiful to the ear. The conductor has to hold everything together. Each instrumentalist must play their particular instrument well, but also in a manner that harmonizes well with the rest of the band.

DR. MC SEZ

Part of the conductor's role is to set the spirit of the church. Pay personal attention to the areas that matter, where the vision is being worked out through gifted people. Here are some realities to remember when recruiting volunteers.

- **Recruiting volunteers is a never-ending job.** In most smaller churches, the pastor is a team of one responsible for recruiting. Help is there in larger churches through recruitment teams or leadership development ministries, but you can't just hope people will volunteer. Keep the conductor's hat nearby.

- **Make the steps or process to serve in your church simple and clear.** Church leaders think people in the congregation understand how to get involved in a ministry, but church people have no idea how to get involved. You must show them how.

- **A tiny percentage of people come and volunteer their service.** An average person feels unqualified to do spiritual work. Others learned from past experience that volunteering for a task often turns into a lifetime assignment. Help them understand they're called to ministry. Invite them to join you in God's work—his mission on earth.

- **Busyness in life has increased.** Most people can give you only two to three hours a week of time in addition to Sunday worship attendance. Between jobs, home, and outside activities, a working couple can easily be busy one hundred hours a week. They aren't less committed, just selective. Use their time wisely.

- **Treat your volunteer teams well.** People who give three or more hours a week volunteering at your church become unpaid staff. Take care of them.

- **The larger the group, the more difficult it is to recruit volunteers.** Think of your church as a congregation of small groups, classes, or other smaller gatherings. Use these smaller groups as a base for recruiting. Face-to-face groups are a source of volunteers in every church.

- **Ministry is a partnership.** As conductor, you are not a boss, and your people are not your employees. The people who serve in your church are your partners. Treat them that way!

- **Show people you care about them.** The more people-oriented you are, rather than program-oriented, the easier it is to recruit and motivate others.

Overcoming the Code Words

Studies over the past three to four decades consistently point out that recruiting and motivating volunteers is one of the top one or two issues facing pastors.[1] Wearing the conductor's hat focuses on these two aspects of church life. You may want to leave the conductor's hat on the rack. Most pastors don't relish the work of recruiting and motivating new volunteers. If you've ever heard someone say, "I'll pray about it," you know that's simply code for "I don't think so." How can you get beyond the code of rejection? Here are some general ideas to consider.

Begin with prayer. At one point in his ministry, Jesus observed how people were distressed without a shepherd. Instead of sending his disciples to meet the people's needs, he called them to prayer. "Beseech the Lord of the harvest to send out workers into His harvest," he told them (Matt. 9:38). This is where you must begin, asking God to raise up workers, leaders, and volunteers so you can fulfill his mission through your church.

Build a solid foundation. Recruiting begins with building a biblical theology of giftedness. Teach others that no one has all the gifts necessary to build a church. Let them know that everyone has at least one spiritual gift to use in serving the body (1 Pet. 4:10). Encourage them to discover their gifts and to start using them.

Analyze your process. Ask questions. Has the church erected conscious or unconscious barriers that discourage people from volunteering? Do people understand the need? Is there a clarity about what is to be done? Is there a support system in place? What is God saying to you through this vacancy? Work hard to discover what possible volunteers are saying beneath the surface when they refuse to participate. For example, are they rejecting the role because they don't like the leader? Or are they too busy? Or are they misunderstanding what the role entails? Talk through the opportunity with them. If you let them talk long enough, and don't stop at their initial rejection, their true reason will become clear. When you find out the real reasons behind the rejection, you'll be able to address them.

Focus on people rather than programs. Examine the church by looking at the various ways the Holy Spirit has designed each person. Imagine how the church might function if the various parts of the body served based on their gifts. Gradually redeploy people who are already volunteering in accordance with their spiritual gifts. As you do, people will become more resistant to burnout, confident they are doing God's will, and fruitful in ministry.

Model off-stage ministry. If you want more people to serve, they need to see you and other leaders in ministry situations up close. To overcome people's reluctance to serve, let them know you experience pain, as well as victory, in ministry. Show them that ministry can grow out of weaknesses as well as strengths.

Trust people with ministry. If you're going to see results from your recruitment, you have to put your reputation, and the church's, on the line. New recruits may not do ministry as well as you or other leaders in the church, but if you don't release control, you'll miss the life-giving power that comes from having others involved in serving. You'll also have to give up feelings of perfection. Yes, you'll want to do ministry so it brings honor to God, but volunteers can't live under the tyranny of perfection. Reasonable mistakes are a price you pay for letting others serve.

Empower those already serving. People will project their own gifts for ministry onto you. Those with a gift for mercy will want you to do more visitation. Those with a gift for prophecy will want you to defend the faith more often in your teaching. Those with a gift of administration will want you to organize the church better. People tend not to be aware of their own abilities as gifts. In fact, what people criticize reveals their own gifts. Your role is not to take on their gifts. Your job is to reflect the gifts back on them and enlarge their confidence to expand their own ministry. Lift up others who are serving. Reward them with much thanks. Ask current volunteers to share stories of how God has worked in their lives through serving. Share their stories live from the stage or via video productions.

Prune for fresh focus. Churches have trouble finding workers or leaders. How often have you heard someone say, "We don't have enough leaders"? If you have more opportunities to serve than people available, don't assume the issue is too few leaders. Perhaps you have too many slots to fill. Churches are often trying to do too much. It's not a recruitment problem but an attempt to do more than is possible. Prune back your ministries and do less, but do it well. Consider streamlining the ministry into sections that can be led by teams rather than individuals. Then build a team based around people's gifts and strengths. This will give each person a support group to help them while taking some aspects of ministry off individual shoulders. Combine competing ministries. Since people often don't or won't give you more than about three hours of time beyond Sunday attendance, make sure ministries aren't overlapping or competing. If two or more ministries are competing for the same participants, see if there is some way to streamline them into fewer ministries. In his story about the vine and the branches, Jesus noted how the healthy branches that brought forth last year's fruit were pruned back to make room for next year's vines. Pruning allows you to focus on what God wants you to do this season, and you'll need fewer workers to do it.

Establish reasonable qualifications. Don't expect volunteers to be elder qualified to get started. All churches desire mature volunteers who are walking closely with the Lord, but the reality is that churches set the requirements to serve so high, hardly anyone can reach them. Remember the qualifications listed in 1 Timothy and Titus are for elders and deacons, not for beginning servants! Get people involved early. It's a little risky, but not doing it poses greater risk. If newcomers sit too long, you actually are teaching them *not* to serve. It's better to recruit newcomers into service quickly—by their third or fourth visit if possible. Ask for their help putting Bibles out on tables, making coffee, setting up chairs, making name tags, or distributing programs and bulletins. Invite them into anything that says, "We want you to serve." Letting newcomers assume some small degree of responsibility says two things: you are valuable and needed.

Invite them to come on mission with you. People want to do something important to make a difference. Replace the request to serve, teach, or manage with a request to help influence the minds and hearts of people for Jesus Christ. Ask them to help win the world, or at least your community, for Christ. Demonstrate the value of the ministry and resist the temptation to downplay it. Install a call-driven ministry model. Help your people discern their own call to ministry. If no one feels called to fill a slot in a current ministry, maybe that ministry is due for closure. Let that ministry die with dignity. Called leaders are passionate. Don't start a new ministry without them.

Finally, give ministries to younger people. Older church leaders are legendary for making comments like, "Why don't the younger people take over? We've done our job." Or, "Younger people today are just not committed." I'm sure you've heard the comments. Possibly, you've made them yourself. Young people have potential for leadership, but they just aren't given an opportunity. This is *keychain leadership*, meaning that whoever holds the keys has the power to let people in or out. Some people hold the keys of ministry tightly, refusing to give them to others. Others loan the keys out but quickly take them back if the new volunteers don't do things the way the key holder likes. Look for younger leaders and give them their own set of ministry keys. Let them do ministry their way, support them, train them, and trust them. They are driven by passion and the opportunity to feel a part of something larger than themselves. Numerous younger people are waiting to be asked.

The Case of the Eager Volunteer. Sally's family started attending Quest church six months ago. Her husband's job required travel away from home two weeks a month, and, with their two elementary-age children in school, she hoped to volunteer at church. In their previous church, Sally sang on the worship team, assisted with the middle school ministry, and mentored some of the teenage girls. She wished to get involved at Quest in similar ways.

One Sunday, Sally noticed a card in the church program asking potential volunteers to indicate an interest by completing the card and placing it in the offering bag. The card stated that some-one from the church would contact her to discuss placement in a ministry. Eagerly, she filled the card out and turned it in that day. When she didn't hear anything the following week, she filled it out again the next Sunday, thinking the first card was misplaced in the church office. She waited an additional three weeks. When she still didn't hear anything, she completed it a third time. After hearing nothing again, she gave up, telling her husband, "I guess they don't need me."

Sally's story is told repeatedly by people who once desired to volunteer but who couldn't get noticed. Gifted people who are successful at their place of employment can't get recruited in their own church. Talented newcomers don't understand how to become involved at their new church. Potential volunteers eager to serve can't get noticed. Their churches should go to MIT.

Go to MIT

I'm not talking about the Massachusetts Institute of Technology. Rather, these churches need to organize a *ministry involvement team* (MIT). Seek out those with a gift of administration and let them wear the conductor's hat. Put in place a team of people who take responsibility for recruiting, training, and placing others in ministry. Think of the MIT as a sort of placement department. The primary task of the MIT is to get to know each individual in your church well enough to know their spiritual gifts, passions, interests, and abilities. This starts by assisting people to take inventory of the resources God has entrusted to them—natural talents, spiritual gifts, and acquired skills—then linking the volunteers with ministry opportunities that fit their resources. Last, the MIT keeps in touch by following up with each volunteer to make certain the fit is a good one. The key to making the MIT work is to keep an accurate list of attendees, have each person fill out a questionnaire and provide basic information, and then have a system to keep that information up-to-date and useable. Most successful churches find that a personal interview of each person, with a follow-up meeting for placement in a ministry, is the most productive approach.

When placing people in a ministry, here are some practices the MIT should follow:

1. **Put people on a team.** Never put someone into a ministry alone. Jesus sent his early disciples out two by two. Their assignment stretched them, taught them new skills, and expanded their understanding of ministry. They may have felt the challenge was too much for them, but going with another person gave them support and encouragement along the way.

2. **Make it easy to serve.** Now, honestly, who wants to get involved with a ministry that is complicated and difficult to grasp? Make the ministry easy to understand. If you can't communicate what you want them to do in about one minute, it's too complicated.

3. **Offer training.** Provide a number of different ways to learn and grow. Give them an article to read, send them to a seminar, assign them to a mentor, but don't send them into ministry without some basic training.

4. **Put a time limit on their service.** Tell them up front to try on the ministry for size. If it fits them, good; but if not, they are free to try on another ministry. Give them a date when you'll sit down and discuss future options together.

5. **Follow up.** Check in to see if the volunteer is finding fulfillment and fruitful ministry. Follow-up should happen three times: at the end of one month of service, again at the end of the third month, and a final check-in at the end of the sixth month.

DR. MC SEZ

Wearing the conductor's hat requires a pastor to motivate others to participate. Finding good motivational tools that work is important for long-term
success. As it turns out, providing incentives—extra pay, awards, praise—is
not the prime motivating factor. The best way to motivate people to serve
well is a bit surprising. It comes when two factors are in place: being on a
team and having a coach. When people are part of a team and feel a sense
of togetherness, they perform better. The reason? They don't want to let
the team down. People who have coaches tend to double or triple their
efforts. Put these two factors together, and you have a powerful mixture
for motivation.

The Rest of the Story

The dark side of many attempts at recruitment in a church is that
it acts like a stimulant. The motivation jolts people into service
for a while but inevitably leaves them drained in the end. Research
on motivation that is sustainable has identified the specific need
for pastors and other leaders to be people of godly character who
practice specific behaviors. Volunteers are motivated when they
are led by people who live what they profess. Such leaders earn
respect and motivate their followers to strive to be like them. Godly
character is not the total story, however. Leaders who motivate
volunteers in sustainable ways are encouragers as well. In practice, volunteers are encouraged when a leader (1) prays with them,
(2) affirms them, (3) meets with them, and (4) appreciates them.
When you wear the conductor's hat, be an encourager.

DR. MC SEZ

A pastor doesn't need to be vocal; in fact, quiet encouragement seems to
work best.[2] Practice some of the following ideas:

- **Make volunteers part of your weekly to-do list.** Add the names of all your volunteers, particularly those who give three or more hours a week to ministry, to an encouragement list. Find a way to encourage at least one of the people on your list each day. Cross the names off your list after you encourage them. When the list is complete, do it again, updating it to include any new volunteers.

- **Make a call.** On the way home from your office, or while traveling anywhere, call one of your volunteers and thank them for serving. If they don't answer the phone, leave a voicemail with your thanks. They'll keep your message on their phone for months.

- **Write a note.** Keep a stack of postcards on your desk where you can't ignore them. At the end of each day, take one minute to handwrite a short note of thanks to a volunteer. It's better than an email, and it will get noticed.

- **Build a habit of saying thank you.** Put three coins in your pocket in the morning. During the day, thank a volunteer in person. Each time you do, move one coin to your other pocket. After a while, you won't need the coins; it'll become second nature to you to thank volunteers. (By the way, don't forget to thank your employed staff too.)

Wearing the conductor's hat is far more important today than it used to be. Quite a number of your people are living on the ragged edge of life. They wonder if you really understand the merry-go-rounds of expectations and responsibilities they face. Most don't have the time or energy to devote to volunteering at church like previous generations once did when dad worked forty hours, mom stayed home, and life was reasonably uncomplicated. Yet, they desire to use their gifts. It's just that, well, they must be careful in the use of their time. Wearing the conductor's hat is crucial to helping people find their way into fruitful service for Jesus Christ. Wear it well.

For Further Reading

Classic: Douglas W. Johnson. *Empowering Lay Volunteers*. Nashville: Abingdon, 1991.

Newer: Sue Mallory. *The Equipping Church: Serving Together to Transform Lives*. Grand Rapids: Zondervan, 2016.

10

The Reporter's Hat

Church life for pastors is lived in a fishbowl. Members of a congregation inspect their pastor's work, life, and play intently, with a proper (or improper) review of their family. Watching the pastoral fishbowl is an old exercise, almost an art in a few churches. Here and now, social media sources are alert for information on pastors too. Churches of larger size are vulnerable to meddlesome investigators who post their presumptuous judgments for the world to see. Investigators have ways of finding out what they want to know, whether you desire them to know or not. Your best choice is to tell them.

You don't need to tell everyone everything. Some matters are for members of the church family only. Other items are properly reserved for private meetings, one-on-one discussions, and the church board. What I'm talking about is the facts important for your church's various publics to know.

Pastors outfit themselves with the reporter's hat by representing the church in the larger community. As churches partner more and more with other churches and nonreligious agencies, pastors are the face of the congregation to the community. The reporter's hat is one of the more important items in the pastor's wardrobe today. The various audiences watching a church will get information some way—whether correctly or wrongly. It's the pastor's job to communicate the right information to those who desire to know it. Pastors of plateaued churches wear the reporter's hat a half hour more per week than those in growing churches but an hour and a half more per week than pastors in declining churches.

The Case of the Confused Community. Reverend Fowler started his first week at the Church of God by walking the neighborhood around the church property, talking with people along the way. He continued this practice for the first month of his new pastorate in order to ascertain how the local community felt about his new church.

One of the constant comments was encapsulated in the words of a middle-aged woman: "When are you going to build on that property you own on the corner? There's been a sign up there for nearly ten years that says, 'FUTURE HOME of the CHURCH of GOD,' but there's nothing on that property but weeds. You folks don't even cut the weeds. It's become an eyesore in the community."

The words echoed through Reverend Fowler's head as he contemplated how his church might possibly reach out to the un-

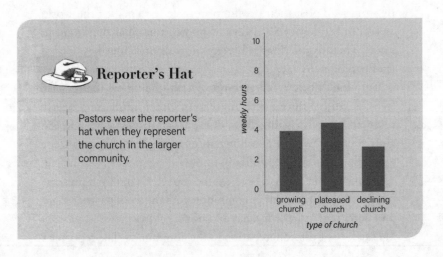

Reporter's Hat

Pastors wear the reporter's hat when they represent the church in the larger community.

weekly hours

growing church · plateaued church · declining church

type of church

churched people in his community. It was obvious that the church's communication to this part of its constituency had not been positive. "How can we communicate better to raise the admiration and trust of people around the church property?" It was an excellent question that needed to be answered.

Define Your Publics

Years ago, pastors thought of only two publics: congregation and community. In general, pastors assumed the constituency that mattered was the congregation. Potent churches recognize a variety of publics. Each expects—requires—individualized communication. Consider how you might communicate information to each of the following publics.

Employees. It's not good if paid staff hear crucial news through the grapevine, over the rumor mill, or after it's announced. If they get most of their information secondhand, it may be untrue or, at a minimum, distorted. At the worst, it'll undermine trust in your leadership. It's of prime importance that you keep your paid employees up-to-date on pertinent information.

Church members. The attitudes and opinions of your committed members matter a great deal. They expect to be kept informed of major plans, changes, and new directions. Internal affairs are of particular interest.

Church attendees. The regular participants at your worship services require knowledge about the larger aspects of your church. What are the church's vision, goals, hopes, plans, and needs? Most don't care about the internal workings of your church, but knowing the larger picture is crucial to their ongoing support.

Parents of children/teens. Growing churches are usually warm nests where parents can raise their children in safety. They await knowledge that affects their children's lives. Changes in leadership (children's or youth pastors) rank high on their need-to-know list.

Instruction about how the church is building character in their young ones and keeping children safe is critical.

Financial supporters. Those who provide regular financial offerings must receive significant news about the financial health of your church before it appears in the financial reports at business meetings. By keeping them informed—truthfully and in a timely way—you'll sustain their confidence and goodwill.

Financial community. Pastors and other church leaders forget that banks, credit unions, and other financial loan companies are a key part of their publics. While churches call upon such organizations only in key situations (e.g., when seeking a building loan), it's important to communicate with them on a timely basis. Building a base of knowledge among these publics goes beyond simple recognition to building trust.

Volunteers. Businesses have shareholders who must be communicated with to maintain their morale and benevolence. Volunteers are much like shareholders, as they invest not only financially in a church but also personally through dedicated service. It's necessary for your volunteers to receive significant information about your church before the general public becomes aware.

Larger community. As a member of the local community, your church's duty is to strengthen and protect it. If you hope to be accepted and supported by the larger community, you'll need the confidence of its members and officials. Not only are you dependent on the community for your safety, sanitation, and health, but you'll also need cooperation when growth requires traffic control and building construction. Moreover, this is the community you've decided to reach with the gospel. It's good sense to provide honest and clear communication to those who live there.

Local community officials. What do community leaders such as the mayor, chief of police, and fire chief understand about your church? Do they see your church as a positive force in the community? Have they even heard of your church? What impressions do they have about your contributions to the greater good?

Target audience. Churches grow and decline according to how well they are able to identify, communicate to, and connect with their target audience(s). Any decision you make affects your outreach success. Thus, it's good to ask, "How will our actions improve or undercut our ability to reach the unchurched in our community?" Whenever you make a decision that will affect your target audience(s), ask, "How can we communicate this in a manner to enhance understanding among those we're trying to reach?"

Suppliers. Churches forget that a network of suppliers provides services and goods that help the church's ministry. Think of the wide network of people who provide services and goods to your church during the year: electrical, telephone, internet, janitorial, gardening, and industrial and commercial services (floor mats, washroom supplies, carpet cleaning, etc.). Proper communication with suppliers builds your credibility in the larger marketplace.

Read the Sentiments of Your Publics

The first task when wearing the reporter's hat is to read the sentiments of your publics accurately. It'll take some time, wisdom, and patience, but you can find out what people are actually thinking and feeling. Steer clear of fast assumptions. Avoid the temptation to assume what you think your publics know or feel. Dig for the truth by doing some of the following.

Start by putting everyone on your research team. Ask key leaders in your church to start listening to what they hear others say about your church. Suggest they ask a barber or hairdresser, a mechanic or shop owner, what they know about your church. Instruct them to not argue or debate anything but simply to listen and catalog what they hear. If they let their emotions take over, they'll stop listening while preparing their rebuttal. Good listening requires a calm demeanor.

Walk around your church's neighborhood. Like Reverend Fowler, you can stop to casually talk with people you meet and ask them what they know about your church. The answers may surprise you, even alarm you, but they also may open your eyes to what your church has been communicating to the larger community over the years. Look at your church's communication through the nonchurched person's eyes.

Make a list of the people who have visited in the last twelve months but not stayed. Send them a brief survey and ask them to share why they chose not to attend on a regular basis. You may hear from only a small number (usually about 10 percent), but what they say is oftentimes informative.

Interview a selection of volunteers, staff, members, attendees, parents, employees, and others to learn what their thoughts are about your church. Where are they confused, misinformed, misguided, or annoyed? What information do they feel is needed for them to do their work or ministry in an excellent way? Use open-ended requests such as, "Tell me about it," "Give me the details," or "Please explain." Repeat what people tell you in their own words so they understand you heard them.

Remember: the place to measure the opinions of your publics is in the marketplace, among your employees, and in conversations with those outside your church. You cannot gauge the attitudes and opinions of your publics while sitting in your desk chair in the pastor's office.

Communicate, Communicate, Communicate

Devise a communication plan. Aristotle reportedly offered some sound advice for communicating well: "Think like a wise man but communicate in the language of the people." The best language is the kind you use when talking informally with your people face-to-face. No matter how busy you are as a pastor, it's best to talk personally with your publics, especially when big changes are in the works. Whenever you have a large change or adjustment to ministry coming in the future, make it a point to stroll through the office or meet with some volunteers, members, attendees, etc., to discuss the subject. This sort of edge-of-the-desk discussion will provide keen insight. When you're sitting on the edge of the desk talking with others, it gives you immediate knowledge of whether they are with you or not, whether they understand or not, and whether they need additional information or not.

Here are some key encouragements you should follow when putting together a communications plan.

First, run from glibness. It never pays to substitute glib announcements for words, ideas, and honest communication. The best advice is to communicate to your publics the way you'd like to be communicated to—clearly. Communicating clearly and honestly to your internal publics is the beginning. It's not always what you say that counts but what they hear and absorb. Be sure to communicate these key issues often.

- Talk about your core values—your vision, purpose, and goals—until everyone on your team down to the lowest level can articulate them to you. You're going to be tempted to quit talking about these core issues long before people really own them. Be sure to refer to at least one core value every week in your message.
- Tell all the people how to find their place in fulfilling the core values of your church. Church attendees often say they don't know how they can help. Be clear on the steps to become involved, use gifts and talents, and serve. Assume everyone desires to serve, and make it plain how to join the team.
- Share the successes you experience in meeting the vision, purpose, and goals. People need to hear the small victories as well as the larger ones. Tell people the good that's happening each week, and tie it to some aspect of your core values.

169

- Point out how lives are being changed through the stories of real people. Let the people tell their own stories. Nothing communicates as personally as personal stories.
- Express and affirm the contributions of people publicly as well as through notes and phone calls. Remember: what gets praised gets done.
- Maintain open and loving connection to people. Communication is a two-way street. You've got to receive communication as well as deliver it.

People in your church must know how the church works, what it values, how to raise concerns, how to commit to service, and how they will be rewarded. The more clearly you communicate in these areas, the better off your church will be.

Second, make everyone in your church a public relations person. Getting as many people as possible to disseminate your church's message is something you must encourage at every opportunity. It's called word-of-mouth advertising. When you have a public relations staff of hundreds or thousands, depending on the size of your church, your message will be empowered to spread through numerous networks. Simple steps, such as providing sharp business cards with an inspirational Scripture and the church's website information on them to everyone in attendance, and then encouraging people to distribute those to others they meet, can do wonders to spread a positive flow of communication to the community. Every preaching series, special event, or key day should be backed up with supportive materials that your people are proud to display and share.

Third, tell your church's story to the community. While you think about your church all the time, it's surprising to discover that people in the larger community rarely think about your church. People who live only a block or two away from church property busily drive by without so much as giving your church an afterthought. To get on their radar, your church needs to tell its story every year to the community. This happens most efficiently through a well-designed website and regular mailings to the homes of people in your community.

DR. MC SEZ

A lot of times bad community relationships boil down to bad communication, and good community relationships boil down to good communication. To improve communication to your community, start with the following realizations:

1. All churches advertise or market themselves. It's not whether you do or don't, but whether you do so poorly or adequately.
2. Advertising and marketing build awareness. These efforts may not get people to come to your church, but they can help the larger community to get to know your church.
3. The best advertising and marketing are tied to people's needs. Thus, it's good to discover the felt needs of the people in the community you serve and to share how your church can help.
4. Advertising and marketing reduce fear and misunderstanding among unchurched people simply by letting people know about the church and pastor.
5. Advertising and marketing alleviate rumors by clarifying for the community what the church is trying to achieve.
6. Advertising and marketing work best when repeated. One-time communication never works, but repetition is a key to getting through to people.

Tell Your Story, and Make It Worth Telling

When wearing the reporter's hat, it's your responsibility not only to tell your church's story but also to make sure the story is worth telling. The church is called primarily to point people to Jesus Christ as the source of salvation. As the church did this throughout

171

history, it also took time to meet the everyday needs of people. When we observe disciples throughout church history, we can see that they were equal parts evangelists and social activists. They demonstrated a zealous commitment to the care of souls (evangelism) and bodies (physical and psychological needs). Balancing an internal care for souls with an external care for bodies demonstrated a holistic attempt to "seek the welfare of the city where I have sent you" (Jer. 29:7).

A church of any size can make a difference not only by caring for people's souls but also by caring for the needs of people in its community. Most churches organize ministries around the desires of publics within the church, but dynamic churches feature an array of outreach ministries—after-school programs, food banks, clothing stores, community development projects, and neighborhood beautification projects, to name just a few—that are built around the needs of those publics outside the church. Some churches continue to frown on the church's engagement in social activism. But while for some a stigma still remains attached to mixing social and sacred activities, many no longer see the problem. In fact, it's fair to ask, "Is my church fulfilling its full purpose if our people do not put what's proclaimed on Sunday into everyday practice?" In ever increasing numbers, pastors are answering no to that question and then leading their churches to engage in more socially active ministry. Here are some ideas for helping your church to have a story that's worth reporting.

- **Be faithful to what God is calling you to do—spiritually and socially.** When you discover an opportunity for ministry outside your church, pray about it. Ask questions: "Am I the right person to lead this initiative?" "Is there another person in my church who is better equipped to take on this project?" "Is there an organization in the community that should run with this idea?" A church must ask, "Is there a need?" "Can we deal with it competently?" "Is anyone else doing it?" "Is this a way we can make a unique contribution?" The church is not here to take care of every problem known to humanity. Know what your mission is and stick to it. Don't get connected to community action projects unless they fit your mission.

- **Define your role in respect to the need you see.** Not everyone is called to take on a particular issue, so you need to define your role. Ask, "How will my involvement in this issue directly impact the lives of those I'm called to serve and those to whom I'm called to witness?" "What is God calling me to do regarding this need?" Knowing which activist tasks to take on is a challenge when wearing the reporter's hat.

- **Link arms with city hall.** Schedule an appointment with a city official to become acquainted. Share your desire to partner with the city to meet the needs of the community. After all, you both serve the same publics. Communicate your church's desire to seek the welfare of the city. Start with whatever tasks you are invited to do and do them in an excellent manner. Slowly build trust over months and years of service.

- **When possible, get involved with school boards, local banks, government agencies, and community organizations.** Be the presence of Christ wherever it's possible, and deliberately carry God's concerns for the lonely leaders in your city who make key decisions that affect the lives of thousands of people.

- **Gain trust by keeping confidences, avoiding criticism, and standing with community leaders in prayerful support.** Through these opportunities, develop friendships with no strings attached.

- **Stay put in your ministry.** A long tenure in one place will make you a sort of bishop of the city—in other words, you'll become known, respected, and trusted by key community leaders. By engaging community leaders for one or more decades, you'll increase your credibility to speak to needs you identify in the city. Not only will you have a seat at the table, but you will also have a voice.

- **Ensure financial integrity.** Business leaders often lack trust in church leaders due to their perception that some churches and Christian ministries have poor financial accountability. Give attention to the fine details of fiduciary responsibility. Make certain your church pays its bills on time. Keep good accounts with your church's local bank and creditors. Be sure to handle your own financial dealings well. The word gets around about your financial savvy.

DR. MC SEZ

Involvement in community activities is a great way to minister outside your church walls. For some pastors, maybe you, it's even more exciting than ministering within the walls. Watch out for the following:

- **Losing credibility at church.** Keep the ministry in your own church a priority. You'll lose trust if you invest too much time away from church. If the ministry within is stumbling along, you have no business serving outside your church. Give attention to serving the people you have so your hard-earned credibility doesn't erode.

- **Losing interest in church.** Growth and change within a church are painstakingly slow. Compared to the fast-paced ministry in partnership with movers and shakers in your community, it's easy to neglect the boring business meeting at church. If you lose interest in your church ministry for the intoxicating work with outside agencies, you'll sabotage your total ministry.

- **Losing focus on God's Word.** Engagement with social agencies in your city may lead you to emphasize social concerns from the pulpit rather than the preaching of God's Word. People need to hear the Bible on Sunday mornings, not your pounding the pulpit about social ills.

- **Losing perspective.** Resist playing the game of "I'll scratch your back if you'll scratch mine." Whatever your involvement in community action initiatives, make certain to do so out of godly concern for people and not the advancement of your own church or ministerial career.

- **Losing vision.** There are so many social ills to invest in solving that it's possible to forget that the primary mission of the church is to preach the atoning work of Christ for salvation. If it is possible to be so spiritually minded that you're of no earthly good, it's equally possible to become so socially minded that you're of no spiritual good. Ask the hard questions, "Am I helping people find Christ?" "Am I seeing lives changed?" "Am I making disciples?"

Your greatest concern must be to call people to eternal life through Jesus Christ. Other organizations can help people with food, clothing, shelter, tutoring, and the like, but *only the church* can offer people eternal life through the *only* Savior Jesus Christ. You must balance your passion to help people with social needs with a passion to see people come to Christ.

Prepare for the Worst

If a catastrophe hit your church tomorrow, would you be prepared for it? Perhaps it could be a newspaper article about a child being molested at your church, a fire that destroys the auditorium, an elder who commits suicide, an employee who embezzles a significant amount of money, or a virus that keeps you from meeting. These are just a few of the occurrences that have, and will, hit churches. If a sudden tragedy were to strike your church, what would you do? Would you know what to tell the community, the church participants, or the press?

Now, I'm not suggesting that you must know ahead of time how to deal with everything, but many pastors have asked, "Why weren't we prepared for this?" It'll serve you and your church leaders well to have a thoughtful procedure ready for handling disasters. As former president Teddy Roosevelt once remarked, "You never have trouble if you are prepared for it." That statement may be overstated, but the basic idea is right—be prepared.

One reason to prepare for the worst is that when a crisis occurs, people will want to know what happened and why. They desire to know what will happen as a result, and what you and other leaders are going to do about it. Furthermore, they want to know now. It's best to be prepared.

When all eyes are focused on you for direction, wearing the reporter's hat is never more essential. You must be ready to tell your story honestly to squash rumors and reduce panic. In most situations, you won't have days or hours to take care of everything that needs to be done. Having a ready-made communication plan in place will buy you time and lessen confusion.

What should be included in your plan? While specific actions and statements must be tailored to the particular situation, the following are some basics.

First, designate specific individuals to speak. Carefully select people to talk to your publics who are emotionally controlled, measured in their words and tone of voice, articulate, and able to bring calm.

Second, determine who will write any published information. Look for those who are excellent writers and able to communicate clearly in written words.

Third, outline a procedure for responding to any and all claims of wrongdoing. As examples, what are the procedures for reporting to authorities and then investigating an accusation of theft, child abuse, or inappropriate touching?

Fourth, designate specific people with key tasks such as contacting legal counsel, insurance agents, proper authorities, and persons involved. Be sure to include in the plan how your church would communicate to every one of your publics. Think through the major questions each public may ask in an emergency. Then prepare a general statement that might be made in such an occurrence.

Being prepared for the worst includes having a plan for how to say, "I'm sorry." Mistakes will be made in any church, and it behooves you to be prepared on how to make a strong apology. A successful apology demonstrates responsibility and acknowledgment of a problem. Most pastors and other church leaders do apologies wrong. The best research suggests there are six components to a good apology that you should keep in mind. First is an expression of regret. Second is an explanation of what went wrong. Third is an acknowledgment of responsibility. Fourth is a declaration of repentance. Fifth is an offer of repair. Last is a request for forgiveness.[1]

Saying "I'm sorry" is a key aspect of wearing the reporter's hat, but it's just one of the aspects. Communication to all the church's various publics is a new hat that numerous pastors are just beginning to take off the rack. It's the glue that holds all of your actions together. Every person in each public needs to know what's taking place in your ministry, what others are doing, and what's being accomplished so they are able to inform others in the church's wide network of influence. Wearing this hat is becoming ever more critical today and will only grow in importance as various communication channels increase in the years ahead.

For Further Reading

Classic: Norman Shawchuck et al. *Marketing for Congregations.* Nashville: Abingdon, 1992.

Newer: Justin Dean. *PR Matters: A Survival Guide for Church Communicators.* N.p.: DOXA Media Group, 2017.

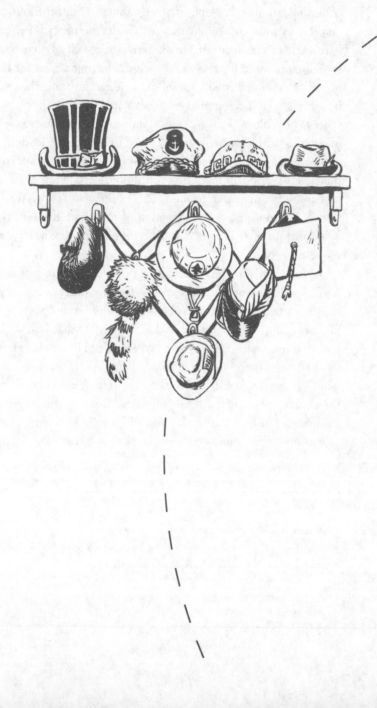

11

The Right-Size Hat

A fruitful pastor must have a hat rack, one with lots of hooks. In the course of ministry, pastors become accustomed to wearing many hats, but no pastor can wear every hat equally well.

My wife and I vacationed in a resort town in the San Bernardino mountains two hours from our home. Strolling along the tiny main street, we noticed a store selling hats—nothing but hats. I soon started trying on hats of various colors and styles, laughing as I looked at myself in a mirror. Some were too small and sat on the top of my head like a toy. Others were scads too large, drooping over my ears. Once I found the right-size hat, it was easy to select ones that fit well. Though the store offered hundreds of hats, only some fit me well, and few looked good on me.

The different hats that pastors wear do not fit equally well on every pastor. A person's different callings, skills, and natural abilities make some hats fit better than others. Learning to change hats is a challenge. Determining which hat or hats you wear best is a pathway to enlarging your ministry and making it more effective. Devoting a little of your time to everything means committing a great deal of yourself to nothing. Your time is a unique resource. Three human resources—time, money, and people—can limit or empower ministry. You can raise more money and find more people, but you can't multiply time. It's limited. So you must narrow your focus and determine which hats you wear best. Start by taking a personal audit of your life and ministry using the following questions.

1. *What did God create me to accomplish? What are my strengths? What am I good at doing?* Have you ever noticed that schools (seminaries too) don't encourage you to focus on your strengths? Instead, they focus on your weaknesses. The homiletics professor says, "You should focus more on explaining the text, because you need help with explaining the text." Why don't we hear, "You should tell more stories. You're really good at story-telling"? This focusing on weaknesses rather than strengths happens throughout our lives, to the point that it's become ingrained for most of us. But experts in leadership development point out how great teachers, leaders, managers, and, yes, pastors recognize strengths and focus on them instead.

2. *Where do I see God's blessing in my life? Where have I seen results?* Be honest and ruthless. Allow me to share a personal example. I wanted to be a preacher, an evangelist, and a musician, but everyone said I was a good teacher. No one was surprised that I ended up teaching in seminary. I also served as a youth pastor, but kids didn't come. In contrast, whenever I worked with adults, my ministry thrived. It was like God was shouting, "*Work with adults!*" With adults, I found success and a great response. No one is surprised I ended up teaching, coaching, and consulting with adults.

To find what God is blessing in your own life, write down what you do, your key activities, and what you hope to see from your activity. Keep a list and then look at it in nine to twelve months. What do you see? The results will show you what God blesses in your ministry. Ask your administrative assistant, if you have one, what you do and don't do well. Ask people around you. If they're honest and have observed you for a number of years, they can tell you. For example, do you seem to be able to recruit and place people well? Do you start new programs that always seem to falter? Where do you sense God's favor in ministry?

3. *What are the key tasks for my church, and are they covered? What needs to be done effectively if this church is to be fruitful?* Sit down with individual leaders from your church and discuss the key activities of your church. Ask them what needs to be done if your church is to be fruitful. Make lists of what each leader tells you. After you've spoken to everyone, look at the lists to see where they overlap. Then look at the few exceptions. Take these outliers seriously, as they may be blind spots that only one person sees. What hats must be worn to serve the needs and opportunities found in your church? What can you do that no one else can do?

Once you have perspectives on these three questions, glance at your hat rack and ask, "What hats should I keep wearing?" "What hats should I start wearing more often, or less often?" "What hats should I stop wearing?" "Which hats should I give to others?" As a pastor, you'll need to wear all the hats, sometimes even the hats that don't fit you so well. Working from your strengths is best, but working from weaknesses is regularly needed.

The United States Olympic hockey team is legendary for winning the gold medal at the 1980 winter games. On their way to winning the gold medal, a team comprised of college and university hockey players unexpectedly beat the Russian national team in a game now called The Miracle on Ice. Coach Herb Brooks told the team, "Play your game. Play your game." He wanted the team to quit trying to be what they weren't and just be themselves. Similarly, pastors need to hear the words, "Wear your hat. Wear your hat." Pastors don't need to wear every hat all the time, but the hats that make them most effective are the ones they should be wearing regularly.

The Case of the Jenga Pastor. Sam Tilton accepted the call to Generation Church a day before he turned twenty-nine years old. Working feverishly, he jumped into the role of pastoring with joy, putting on and taking off the various hats of a pastor with ease. Throughout the next decade, he built his church from a handful of people to two hundred dedicated souls. That's when it all came crashing down like a Jenga game.

Jenga is a Swahili word meaning "to build." This popular game involves building a tower of small bricks in rows of three that are crisscrossed on top of each other, then carefully taking out one brick at a time until one poor soul—the loser—causes the entire Jenga tower to collapse. Throughout the decade, Pastor Tilton had assembled his church like a tower of Jenga blocks. He'd done it by wearing all of a pastor's hats. Youthful energy gave him the grit to put on and take off all the hats quickly and successfully during his early years at the church. But by the end of the decade, the joy of ministry came crashing down. He could no longer handle juggling so many hats. He had become the Jenga pastor, building a church on his own, and then seeing it collapse when he could no longer wear all the hats well. A Jenga pastor suffers from vocational amnesia. Such pastors don't know who they are or what they are supposed to be about, so they try to do everything.

Prioritize Your Hats

Instead of trying to wear all the hats, fruitful pastors prioritize which hats they wear. Here's the amount of hours pastors spend each week wearing the various hats.

Hat	Growing	Plateaued	Declining
Speaker	10	7	5
Captain	9	6.5	5
Coach	9	6	6
Executive	8	7.5	6
Director	8	7.5	6
Counselor	7	6.5	5
Student	7	7	5
Pioneer	6	4.5	3
Conductor	6	7.5	4
Reporter	4	4.5	3
Total weekly hours	**74**	**64.5**	**48**

A close friend of mine collects hats. At last count, he has 182 types, styles, and colors of hats from around the world. When I headed out for vacation last year, I asked him if he'd like me to bring him anything. You guessed it. He replied, "Just a hat."

Now, I don't have as many hats as my friend. I have maybe eight or ten. The odd thing is I mostly wear just one hat. That one hat is important to me, as it reflects important values in my life. Others just hang on the rack. Like me, pastors tend to wear some hats more often than others. Here are some insights.

First, pastors of growing churches work 54 percent more hours on average than do pastors of declining ones. Evidently, it takes more time to lead a growing church than a declining one. Perhaps this is related to the number of people in the congregation or the possibility that pastors of declining churches are bivocational. Whatever the reason, there is some correlation between growth and the amount of time invested and the results of growth.

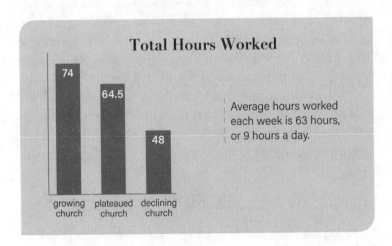

Second, where pastors spend their time is important. It's not just the amount of time invested but where that time is invested that correlates with a church's growth. Pastors in growing churches prioritize the speaker's hat (preaching), captain's hat (leading), and coach's hat (training). Together they wear these three hats 75 percent more than do pastors in declining churches. It might be wise for pastors of declining churches to put more time into wearing these three hats.

Third, while neither pastors in growing churches nor those in declining churches give a lot of time to evangelism (the pioneer's hat), those in growing churches wear the pioneer's hat twice as much. There are only two hats that pastors in growing churches wear twice as often as those in declining ones: the speaker's hat and the pioneer's hat. Pastors in declining churches might do well to focus on improving their speaking ministry and improving their outreach into the community.

Fourth, pastors serving declining churches prioritize the director's hat (discipling), coach's hat (training), and executive's hat (administration). They evidently get entangled in aspects of church governance more than those in growing churches do. Pastors of growing churches may have paid staff members to take care of many administrative details, while those in declining churches end up doing much administration themselves. It's also notable that those in declining churches spend less time communicating (speaker's hat) and casting vision (captain's hat).

Fifth, pastors in both growing and declining churches indicate that they wear the reporter's hat the least. While community involvement is gaining interest in all churches and faith families, it appears to be lagging as a priority in most pastors' agendas.

DR. MC SEZ

Pastors don't know how many hours they work. They find it difficult to separate what they do; ministry overlaps too much to do so. Thus, most overestimate their actual hours worked each week. On average, the number of hours pastors say they work is significantly larger than what they might record in a diary. My research shows that pastors work an average of sixty-three hours a week wearing the ten hats. Pastors who lead numerically growing churches typically spend seventy-four hours in some aspect of ministry work each week. Those leading churches in decline average just forty-eight hours a week on ministry tasks. Thus, pastors in growing churches put in 52 percent more time each week than do those in declining ones. As in most professions, success (or fruitfulness) is linked to hard work. Pastoral ministry is a unique work in that no one tracks a pastor's time. Pastors rarely punch time clocks. They can either work hard or hardly work. I think a majority of pastors put in honest work in ministry, but they don't always invest their time in the aspects of ministry that produce results. The problem isn't inactivity; the problem is spending time in the wrong areas.

How many hours should a pastor work? One way to look at this is to ask how many hours a dedicated layperson who is employed volunteers at your church. Then add forty hours to that. As an example, if the average person volunteers eight hours a week at your church, you should work at least forty-eight hours. If they volunteer twelve hours a week, you should work fifty-two hours. Here's another way to compare a pastor's time involvement to dedicated volunteers. View yourself as working five days a week (Monday–Friday), taking one day off (Saturday), and then volunteering on Sunday. Doing so may give you a different perspective on your work week.

Where should pastors put their time? It's not an easy question to answer given the differences among pastors, congregations, locations, etc. One thing is certain: to lead a growing church, research reveals it's best to put most time into wearing the speaker's hat (preaching and communicating well), the pioneer's hat (investing in evangelism and innovative new ministries), the coach's hat (developing leaders and sharing ministry), and the captain's hat (setting direction and communicating vision). Pastors in growing churches spend twice as much time wearing these four hats as do those pastors in declining ones.

OSTEAK

It's vitally important for a pastor to disappear once in a while in order to gain perspective. Designing a personal plan to get outside of your regular routine to look in the mirror at the hats you are wearing is a good practice. This is OSTEAK—*obvious stuff that everyone already knows*—but it's uncommonly practiced.

As a pastor, I disappeared each week on Tuesday mornings into the deep recesses of the public library. No one knew where I was except for my secretary and wife, which was important in case of emergencies. I sat there in silence, sometimes planning the future, occasionally searching for sermon illustrations, but always reflecting on my practice of ministry. One time I picked up a sports magazine and experienced an OSTEAK moment. As I was reading a story about baseball pitchers, it dawned on me that all teams have a star pitcher, usually the one who pitches the first game of the season or of the playoffs. What struck me was a realization that the star pitcher doesn't play first base, or outfield, or even pitch every game. Multiple players are on the team, all wearing their own hats. Why, even the ball boys and bat girls wear hats. This discovery opened my eyes to see how I was often trying to wear hats that weren't mine to wear, but this sudden realization wouldn't have happened unless I'd disappeared—gotten away from the office to the library to reflect on ministry.

I'm convinced that you need to disappear on a regular time schedule too. Here's how to do it. First, schedule a time to disappear. Find the best day and time to be away from your office. Second, alert key colleagues and family. Let them know where you'll be, and work out any scheduling issues your absence may create. Third, remind everyone one week before you disappear that they shouldn't look for you at that time. Your staff and congregation won't believe you're leaving the office, so give them two warnings. Fourth, leave your cell phone and computer in the office, at home, or at minimum in your car. Fifth, take along only a notebook, some snacks or lunch, and something to drink. Sixth, take a deep breath and vacate completely to a local park, library, picnic grounds, hotel lobby, coffee shop, or anywhere you can have space to think.

Once you've disappeared, pray and think about the hats you're wearing each week. Ask and answer some of the questions found in this book. Jot down your ideas, thoughts, and insights. Resist the urge to edit your notes. Just get them down on paper. Give yourself time and space to think, apart from the pressures and noise of ministry. Then, reflect on Christ's example found in John 17:4. While praying, Jesus distilled the core of his ministry in one simple statement: "I glorified You on the earth, having *accomplished the work* which You have given Me to do" (emphasis added). You've got to do the work God has given you to do; there is no other way to bring glory to him. So, what are the hats you must wear? Which might you give to others? Which must hang on the rack for another time?

DR. MC SEZ

In the final analysis, pastors enjoy ministry and working in multiple areas—at least it doesn't get boring. Here are a few tips I've noticed about pastors who tend to be highly fruitful.

- **They take care of themselves.** They limit their work to reasonable levels, say, about fifty-five to sixty hours a week, consistently take off one full day a week, use all of their vacation each year, and learn to live with unfinished business.

- **They think more about how they invest their time than about how much time they use.** Focusing on a few priorities, i.e., wearing a few hats well, is more important than how much time is spent working each week. It's the concentration of energy that gets results.

- **They find the key log.** In the old days when loggers encountered a logjam on a river, a person would climb a hill or another tree to observe the jam, picking out the key log to remove. Once the key log was removed, the river did the rest, releasing the remainder of the logs downstream. Similarly, effective pastors find the essence of each hat, decide what needs to be done, and do it.

- **They involve others, allowing them to wear the hats too.** The most effective pastors are not those who can wear all the hats well but pastors who can mentor others to wear the hats better than they can. They use a little selective hesitation, thinking about who can wear the hat better than they can before putting on a hat. They ask, "Whose hat am I wearing? Is it my hat or someone else's hat?" If the hat belongs to someone else, they take it off their rack and give it back to the person to whom it belongs.

- **They know what their job is and what hats they should be wearing.** Rather than asking, "How much can I do?" they ask, "What should I do?" It's an entirely different question. It's like the pastor who went around turning out the lights and locking the doors in the church. Is that the hat a pastor ought to wear? Successful pastors know the difference.

- **They set priorities.** They determine which hats are the most important to wear and which are best left on the rack to be worn by others or worn only in emergencies. Successful pastors don't approach ministry like eating at a smorgasbord—sampling a little of everything. Instead, they determine priorities, selecting the hats that fit them best or the hats that will bring the most value to the church or ministry.

Pastors Have Nails

Pastors typically dislike talking about success. They prefer to talk about faithfulness, feeling they can be faithful without being successful. I'm not sure one can remove faithfulness from success, but that's a discussion for another time. Another, and maybe more helpful, way to think about wearing the pastor's ten hats is to think of it as obedience. I'm told that Brazilians describe a person who stays with a task using the word *garra*. The word literally means "fingernails." If a person has *garra*, they have nails, that is, they hang in there. Most of us would call it tenacity or grit.

No pastor goes through a week, or even a day, without wearing multiple hats. Some hats fit better than others, but all hats are worn occasionally. Wearing numerous hats quickly creates a whiplash syndrome, as the hats don't come neatly separated, with breathing space factored in between. While wearing many hats is expected, it means pastors feel pressure to get things done that may be outside their ability. The pressure doesn't typically come from the board or even the congregation. No, the real pressure comes from the person they see in the mirror every morning. All pastors tend to wear too many hats without taking time to gain perspective and make corrections in their work. The healthiest pastors take time to step back from their schedule and reflect by asking probing questions: What did I do yesterday that mattered? How did I waste my time? Did I wear hats I shouldn't have worn? Am I giving energy to the right areas?

John Wooden, the famous basketball coach, encouraged his players, "Be at your best when your best is needed."[1] That is a great statement to remember for pastors too. Whatever hat you wear, wear it well. Be at your best when your best is needed.

Worksheet

An old story tells of a lumberjack who worked each day on sharpening his saw before going out to work among the trees. He found that the time spent sharpening his saw resulted in more efficient cutting. What hats do you need to wear better? Look over the list of hats on the next page and check each one as Sharp, Needs Sharpening, or Dull. Which three hats do you need to sharpen this year?

Ten Hat Saws to Sharpen

Speaker's Hat	☐ Sharp	☐ Needs Sharpening	☐ Dull
Captain's Hat	☐ Sharp	☐ Needs Sharpening	☐ Dull
Coach's Hat	☐ Sharp	☐ Needs Sharpening	☐ Dull
Executive's Hat	☐ Sharp	☐ Needs Sharpening	☐ Dull
Director's Hat	☐ Sharp	☐ Needs Sharpening	☐ Dull
Counselor's Hat	☐ Sharp	☐ Needs Sharpening	☐ Dull
Student's Hat	☐ Sharp	☐ Needs Sharpening	☐ Dull
Pioneer's Hat	☐ Sharp	☐ Needs Sharpening	☐ Dull
Conductor's Hat	☐ Sharp	☐ Needs Sharpening	☐ Dull
Reporter's Hat	☐ Sharp	☐ Needs Sharpening	☐ Dull

Top Three Hats to Sharpen

1. _____

2. _____

3. _____

The Study

The study noted in *The 10 Key Roles of a Pastor* is based on the results of a twelve-question survey designed, distributed, and compiled on the Survey Monkey platform. A total of 197 lead or solo pastors completed usable surveys between June 2019 and August 2019 for a confidence level of 94 percent (+/– 6 percent). Answers were self-reported, and it is assumed questions were answered honestly. However, students of survey design will note that self-reporting usually involves a halo effect, wherein answers are notably embellished.

Church size was indicated by the number of worshipers the week before the survey was taken: small churches (200 or fewer), medium churches (201–800), large churches (801–2,000), and megachurches (2,001 or more). Growth, plateauing, or decline was determined by comparing worship attendance from the week before the survey was taken to five years ago. No specific percentage of growth or decline was required, but just a simple increase or decrease in attendance from five years before.

A copy of the survey is available by emailing the researcher at cgnet@earthlink.net.

It is recognized that pastors wear other hats that were not in-cluded in the survey research. For example, readers may wonder about the family hat or the prayer hat. These, and other possible hats (e.g., personal care), were left out of the survey in an attempt to focus on what pastors actually do in directly serving a church. Thus, the survey was not strictly a time management survey but

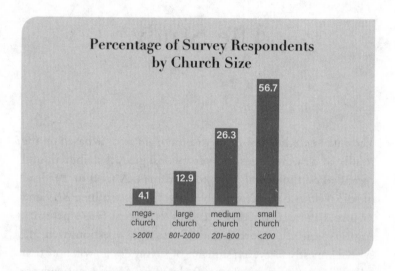

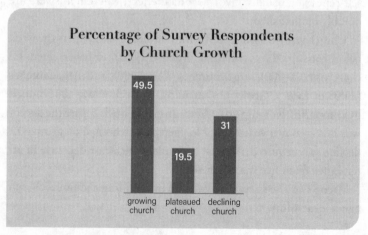

more of a functional survey based on the major areas (hats) that engage a pastor's time at work. The majority of pastors are both male and married. However, no attempt was made to determine the gender or marital status of reporting pastors. A pre-survey study assisted in determining what aspects of pastoral ministry were included in each of the ten hats.

Notes

Chapter 1 The Speaker's Hat

1. "The Pulpit's Personal Side: A Leadership Forum," *Leadership Journal*, Spring 1990, 21.

2. Donald R. Sunukjian, "The Credibility of the Preacher," *Bibliotheca Sacra* 139 (July 1982): 264.

3. Charles Arn, "Remember the Pastor's Message Three Weeks Ago?," *Church Growth Network*, November 2000, 1.

Chapter 2 The Captain's Hat

1. Lyle E. Schaller, *The Multiple Staff and the Larger Church* (Nashville: Abingdon Press, 1980), 108–16.

2. Okay, that was too personal. Yet, a close friend of mine who leads national pastoral training seminars often asks that question of pastors. He has them write yes or no on a small piece of paper and turn it in. The results of this admittedly unscientific poll found 90 percent of pastors saying no.

3. Another word that is often used interchangeably with purpose is *mission*. I see purpose and mission as essentially the same.

Chapter 5 The Director's Hat

1. Charles Schulz, *Peanuts*, November 27, 1977, https://www.gocomics.com /peanuts/1977/11/27.

Chapter 6 The Counselor's Hat

1. Carl F. George, "Beyond the Firehouse Syndrome," *CT Pastors*, May 19, 2004, https://www.christianitytoday.com/pastors/leadership-books/visionplan ning/lldev02-15.html.

Chapter 7 The Student's Hat

1. Edgar Dale, *Audiovisual Methods in Teaching*, 3rd ed. (New York: Dryden Press, 1969). Edgar Dale completed a study in 1969 that compared the effectiveness of different types of learning. Called the "Cone of Learning," it has been adapted multiple times throughout the years. However, it consistently shows that, after two weeks, people tend to remember just 10 percent of what they hear but 90 percent of what they do.

2. First identified by Russian psychologist Lev Zygotsky as the Zone of Proximal Development (1935), the concept states that people learn as they are guided by those who are more knowledgeable. The concept has influenced education and is used to develop leaders in numerous fields such as the military, wilderness survival, and business management. One modern approach identifies three zones: green (Comfort Zone), red (Stretch Zone), and ultraviolet (Panic Zone). For a simple introduction, see Jacob Goldstein, "Know Your Zone: Pushing Yourself and Your Team to Step Beyond the Comfort Zone," The Leadership Laboratory blog, January 31, 2019, https://www.leadershipdevelopmentlab.com/blog/2019/4/14/know-your-zone-pushing-yourself-and-your-team-to-step-beyond-the-comfort-zone.

3. Peter F. Drucker, *Managing Oneself* (Boston: Harvard Business Review Press, 2015), 36.

4. Warren Bennis and Burt Nanus, *Leaders: The Strategies for Taking Charge* (New York: Harper & Row, 1985), 69.

Chapter 8 The Pioneer's Hat

1. This percentage is my own calculation drawn from recent studies of evangelism and church attendance published by the Barna Group, Lifeway Research, and Pew Research.

Chapter 9 The Conductor's Hat

1. For one example, see Fred Boyce, "Twelve Church Management Problems," *Leadership Journal*, Fall 1982, 72.

2. Scott Berinato, "If You Want to Motivate Someone, Shut Up Already," *Harvard Business Review* 91 (July 2013): 24–25.

Chapter 10 The Reporter's Hat

1. Research by Roy Lewicki, professor emeritus of management and human resources at Ohio State University, as reported by Lance Frazer in "All Apologies," *Costco Connection*, February 2020.

Chapter 11 The Right-Size Hat

1. John Wooden and Jay Carty, *Coach Wooden's Pyramid of Success* (Grand Rapids: Revell, 2009), 21.

Gary L. McIntosh is professor of Christian ministry and leadership at Talbot School of Theology, Biola University, where he teaches courses in the field of pastoral theology. Dr. McIntosh has received several awards, most recently the Lifetime Achievement Award (July 2018) from Church Leader Insights and the Win Arn Lifetime Achievement Award from the Great Commission Research Network (October 2015).

Dr. McIntosh has thirty-eight years of experience consulting with nonprofit organizations, coaching leaders, and giving seminar presentations. He has analyzed over twelve hundred churches representing more than ninety denominations throughout the United States, Canada, Southeast Asia, and Australia. His articles have appeared in numerous publications. He is editor of the *Growth Points Leadership Letter*, and he has written or coauthored twenty-six books, among which are *Overcoming the Dark Side of Leadership* (1998), *One Size Doesn't Fit All* (1999), *Staff Your Church for Growth* (2000), *Biblical Church Growth* (2003), *Beyond the First Visit* (2006), *Taking Your Church to the Next Level* (2009), *There's Hope for Your Church* (2012), *Being the Church in a Multi-ethnic Community* (2012), *What Every Pastor Should Know* (2013), *Donald A. McGavran: A Biography of the Twentieth Century's Premier Missiologist* (2015), *Growing God's Church* (2016), and *Building the Body* (2017).

Gary and his wife, Carol, reside in Temecula, California. They have two grown children and seven grandchildren. Dr. McIntosh is available for speaking or consulting. For information, please contact Dr. McIntosh at Talbot School of Theology, 13800 Biola Ave., La Mirada, CA 90639, or The Church Growth Network, PO Box 892589, Temecula, CA 92589-2589 (951-506-3086). He may also be reached by email at cgnet@earthlink.net.

Connect with
GARY

ChurchGrowthNetwork.com

drgmcintosh

REACHING A CHANGING WORLD WITH THE UNCHANGING GOSPEL

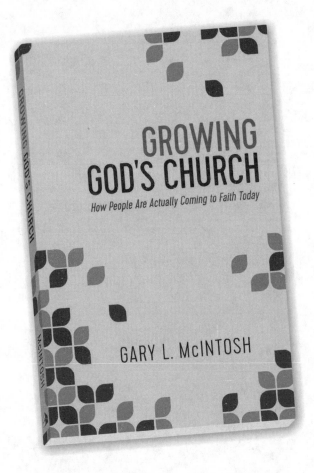

Based on ten years of comprehensive research,
Growing God's Church unveils how people are actually
coming to faith in the twenty-first century.

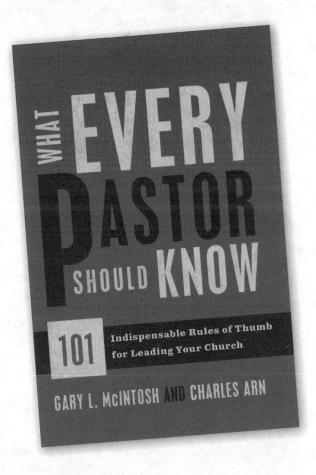

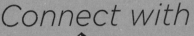